I Can Cook Vegan

I Can Cook Vegan

Isa Chandra Moskowitz

Abrams, New York

I Can Cook Vegan

Intro

After a few decades of writing cookbooks, I think I'm beginning to get it. People want streamlined recipes with easy-to-follow instructions and accessible ingredients.

Is that about right?

Great, then let's proceed!

When I first started cooking, I thought the vegan world needed something a little more adventurous than lentil stew. I'd use ingredients you've never heard of from specialty stores you've never been to. But how things have changed! Tofu is now the other white meat, and even your uncle puts nutritional yeast on his popcorn. That might not be totally statistically accurate, but let's say households are cooking vegan a few times a week, more people than ever are going completely vegan, and everyone is warming up to the idea of cashew cream.

Even I have changed. I want my meals to be fast and easy but still the best food ever. If I want to be adventurous, I've got two restaurants where I can experiment. But this cookbook is for my true love: the home cook. I learned to cook from cookbooks, recipe by recipe, and that's what inspired this book. What if each chapter was a building block to becoming a better, more competent cook? Like learning a new instrument: You master a couple of chords then start putting them together to form songs. Or learning a new language and your vocabulary keeps improving. Or finding your way around a new city. Or . . . well, you get the idea!

Each chapter starts with a fresh mission. So cook your way through, meal after delicious meal, building knowledge and skills as you go. And, of course, you can skip around, too. You do you!

Who Is This Book For?

This book is for cooks of all stripes, but I had a few specifics in mind.

The just-born, brand-new cook

If you're learning to cook, then cooking vegan is the way to go because it's more pleasant to work with chickpeas than chickens. Whether you're 13 or 301 (and a vampire), you might just be starting out. Maybe you're leaning into it with nothing but eagerness and excitement, in which case, cool, go ahead and get started, read no further. But if you're a little hesitant, please remember that this book was written for you by someone who once was you. Sleep with the pages under your pillow and take it one day at a time.

The tried-and-true seasoned cook who is tofu-curious

Maybe you learned to cook from your parents, or maybe you can make a soufflé and boeuf bourguignon, but maybe you only know how to do it with eggs, meat, and heavy cream. Well, if this sounds like you, welcome to vegan cuisine! Here you will learn how to milk a cashew and turn tofu into fish. Have fun with it and keep an open mind. At least some of the tricks you already know will come in handy, and you'll pick up some new knowledge along the way.

The busy weeknight pantry cook

Perhaps this describes everyone? But if you're making spaghetti and meatballs with sauce from a jar and frozen meatless meatballs, you might want to get fresher without too much fuss. Rejoice! These recipes are made with pantry-friendly ingredients that you can always have around. Yes, it will be more work than opening a few packages, but as you get used to it, the effort won't be much harder, and the rewards will be worth it!

The farmers' market junkie who looks at all the pretty colors

You're into food. You Instagram bunches of beets (and your manicure). Yet most of your pretty pics are of avocado toast or grain bowls from that macrobiotic restaurant. You might know a few vegan basics, and you already have a love of vegetables, but get ready to turn your influencer level to *100!*

The reluctant parent to the vegan child

Did your kid just sit you down and deliver the news? No more meat and dairy, Dad. Oy vey. What about Mawmaw's lasagna? Or that French toast that took you one hundred Sundays to perfect? Listen, it's going to be okay. Food is food! You aren't going to have to cook separate

14

meals; you are going to start loving lentils and cooking them alongside your family. When I first went vegetarian as a teenager, my mom got me a bunch of cookbooks, and that's what really brought us together. I hope this can be that book for your family!

Last, for all you lazy vegans doing it for the animals, all you Grubhub addicts, and everyone who saw something about eating plant-based for your health on a talk show, I see you! And you *can* cook vegan.

How to Succeed at Cooking Without Really Trying

1 Read the recipe from beginning to end, have a good understanding of the steps involved, and make sure you have the ingredients and equipment ready to use before starting the recipe. That includes everything from ingredients to blenders to measuring spoons. The French call this *mise en place*. I call it "pile of stuff."

2 Control your heat. Food doesn't burn itself! Most recipes require low to medium heat, but if you are turning it up to boil, always keep a watchful eye and remember to stir. If the pot is too hot, you can turn the heat all the way off and give it a minute. Sometimes it's the most obvious stuff that we *Homo sapiens* forget ever since Peking man discovered fire.

I Can Cook Vegan

Intro

3 Improve your knife skills. The more you prep food, the more you will get the hang of how to handle a knife. You're not aiming to be a sushi chef here (or are you?)—the goal is to get the job done quickly and with some finesse. Watch YouTube videos of people chopping onions and garlic or any veggie that you need to dice. Watch cooking shows. Find the knife that is comfortable for you, and make sure it is always sharp. Most kitchen stores have a sharpening service you can use a few times a year.

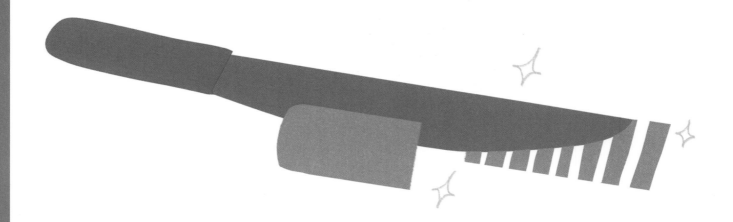

4 Clean as you go. I hate hearing that because I love making messes, but it's so true. Keep a little bowl nearby for scraps. Have a clean wet towel to wipe surfaces. Don't let all that tomato sauce you just spilled get tracked all over the house. Be aware of your surroundings. An organized environment is conducive to cooking, especially for new cooks. You don't want to be overwhelmed with a mess when you're done, or you might never cook again!

Ingredients & Philosophy

A phrase you'll hear me say a lot is "pantry-friendly." And that doesn't just mean cans of chickpeas and packages of rice (although those things certainly count). I use about twenty ingredients over and over in this cookbook to make sure you have lots of options with short recipe lists. So, this book is based on staples that might be lurking in your cupboard or fridge. Most of the veggies are easy to find in any supermarket—I use a lot of broccoli in all kinds of ways.

However, there might be a few ingredients you aren't familiar with, or some that you are familiar with but we are using in a brand-new way. I call those "weirdo ingredients." Here they are.

Kala namak

A salt that tastes like eggs. Yep, it exists, and it makes cooking so much fun! It is also called "Himalayan black salt," but please don't be fooled. For one thing, it is pink. Many other salts are called "black salt," but that doesn't mean they have an eggy flavor. Look specifically for kala namak to ensure it will get the job done. I usually order it online. It's such a yummy ingredient. Besides using it in recipes, I love to sprinkle it on avocado toast or fresh-from-the-vine tomatoes.

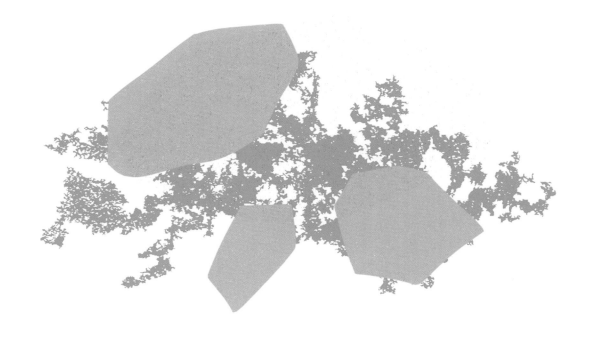

Nutritional yeast flakes

Also called "nooch." They have a nutty, cheesy flavor and can be used in so many ways! Add to stews en masse for cheesiness and creaminess, or in smaller quantities for a little bit of thickening and an umami punch. In baked tofu they give a little extra crispy texture. Or sprinkle them on salads and popcorn like a cheese.

I Can Cook Vegan

Vital wheat gluten & seitan

Vital wheat gluten is the high-protein flour from wheat used to make seitan and sausages and all sorts of fabulous wheat meats. I use Bob's Red Mill Vital Wheat Gluten in all the recipes, and that seems to be the most common one on supermarket shelves. While we're at it, you might want to know what seitan is. It was invented by monks in the mid-twentieth century by washing all the starch out of wheat. How did they figure that out? Who knows, but now we can eat amazing, chewy, grilled cruelty-free meat, so thank you!

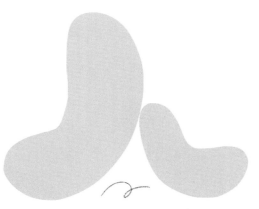

Cashews

Yes, you know what cashews are. But did you know that they could be transformed into a thick, luscious cream akin to heavy cream? The cashews we use to create cream are specifically whole, unroasted cashews, because the flavor is too nutty if they are roasted. And cashew pieces, although way cheaper, can be bitter. Purchase ones that are labeled "raw," "unroasted," or "whole cashews." And make sure they aren't salted. Many recipes in this book call for cashew cream to be made in a high-speed blender (Vitamix or Blendtec). That will take all of one minute. However, if you don't have a high-speed blender, that's no problem! There are a

I Can Cook Vegan

few options to get your cashews creamy and dreamy. Note that an average blender could take anywhere from 2 to 5 minutes to work its charm. Always use a rubber spatula to scrape down the sides, and remember to give your blender motor a break every minute or so to ensure it doesn't burn out.

1.   Soaking. At least a few hours ahead of time (even a day in advance), place cashews in a bowl and cover with a few inches of water. That's it! Then drain and proceed with the recipe.

2.   If you forget to soak, then boil them for 15 minutes.

3.   If you forget to soak and you don't hate micro-waves, place in a microwave-safe bowl, sub-merge in a few inches of water, and heat on high for 2 minutes, then soak for 15 minutes or so.

Tofu

All the savory recipes call for extra-firm tofu. As the name suggests, it's got a firm, chewy texture that you can really sink your teeth into! Sometimes I suggest pressing the tofu, too. That's when you really want a lot of chewy bite.

To press your tofu, remove it from the package and wrap in a paper towel. Then, wrap in a kitchen towel. Now place a few heavy objects, like three or four Guy Fieri cookbooks, on top. The water will start to absorb into the towel and all over your counter. Do this for about an hour, flipping halfway through. Your tofu is now chewier and ready to soak up more flavor. Note: I don't do this for every recipe (some depend on that extra moisture), so press only when needed.

Nori

You're familiar with it in sushi, but I use it like a seasoning to get fishy (but not too fishy) flavors. Grind it into a powder or rip it to bits for a little taste from the sea.

Chapter

Pastas & Noodles

Mission: This chapter will get you multitasking and keep you mindful of timing, without risking too much on anything fancy. It will also give your spice rack a workout and get your pantry stocked with some basics so that dinner is always within reach.

Pasta is, by far, the first thing a home cook reaches for when they want a delicious meal on the table in record time. So what better place to begin? Even if there are a few components (sauce, proteins, what have you), the main component (hello, noodles) is pretty much done for you. And with a little practice and this handy book, the timing will always work out perfectly. From mac and cheese to pad Thai (pages 34 and 48), there is a world of carb-y amazingness out there to explore!

Equipment must-haves

Large pot (6-quart/5.7 L)
Pasta spoon
Large colander

Salting pasta water

The addition of salt to pasta water is really for flavor. The water should be as salty as the sea! But if that's too vague for you, 4 quarts (3.8 L) of water requires a heaping tablespoon of fine sea salt. If that sounds like a lot, don't worry! Most of it goes back out to sea when you drain the pasta.

Pastas & Noodles

Broccoli Mac and Cheese

Mac and cheese. Let's not waste time with formalities. This is obviously the first recipe you will be turning to, so no need to flip through the pages. It easily tops the list of things we can't live without, right after oxygen and cat videos. So what's up with *vegan* mac and cheese? The short answer for the twenty-first century: cashews and nutritional yeast. Those are ingredients I use often to achieve creamy cheesiness, so let's get familiar with them—stat. I love this particular recipe for new vegan cooks because the most important part (the sauce, duh) needs no cooking and takes about 2 minutes to pull together. It also includes my favorite vegetable, broccoli. (Yes, I am that basic.) It's chopped into small pieces and available in every creamy, dreamy bite. The method is also really simple and features every cook's favorite: "one pot." You simply add the broccoli to the pasta in the last few minutes of cooking. So yeah, this is a great place to start. It's really perf served with 2 tablespoons of Noochy Baked Tofu (page 281). I like a little smoky heat, but if you aren't down with that, try smoked paprika instead of the chipotle powder. And if you are not even down with a little smoke, try regular paprika. But that will make you a very boring person!

Ingredients

Serves 6 to 8

1   pound (455 g) pasta (chiocciole, medium-size shells, or, ya know, macaroni)
6   cups (425 g) finely chopped broccoli

For the cheese sauce

1   cup (120 g) whole unroasted cashews (if you don't own a high-speed blender, see page 24)
1   cup (240 ml) vegetable broth
¼   cup (35 g) nutritional yeast flakes
¼   teaspoon ground turmeric
1   tablespoon fresh lemon juice
¾   teaspoon chipotle powder (see headnote)
1   tablespoon onion powder
¼   teaspoon salt

1. In a large pot, bring 4 quarts (3.8 L) of salted water to a boil for the pasta.

2. While the water is coming to a boil, make the sauce: Place all the sauce ingredients in a high-speed blender and blend for about a minute or until completely smooth, using a rubber spatula to scrape down the sides every 20 seconds or so.

3. Cook the pasta in the boiling water for about 5 minutes, then add the broccoli. Boil until the pasta is cooked, stirring often with a slotted pasta spoon, 3 to 5 minutes.

4. Drain the pasta in a large colander and immediately return it to the pot. It should still be piping hot and wet with the cooking water. Do not rinse and do not wait. This part is important because you need the wet, hot pasta to help make the sauce creamy and awesome and cling to the noodles.

5. Add the sauce to the pasta pot and use the rubber spatula to blend. Turn the heat on low and stir for about 2 minutes to get everything warmed through. Taste for salt and seasoning, then serve.

I Can Cook Vegan

Angel Hair Tapenade with Tofu and Arugula

For those of us who want to slather ourselves *and* our pasta in olives, this is the recipe. The sauce is super olive-y, of course, like a nice savory bite of the Mediterranean, but it also has a Parmesan undertone from the miso and nutritional yeast. If you didn't have time to plan ahead and press the tofu, just toss some chickpeas or white beans in when you're adding the pasta to the sauce.

For the grilled tofu

1	(14-ounce/400 g) block extra-firm tofu, drained and pressed (see page 26)
½	cup (120 ml) vegetable broth
2	tablespoons olive oil
2	tablespoons balsamic vinegar
2	tablespoons tamari
2	teaspoons Italian or pizza seasoning blend

For the tapenade

3	cloves garlic
3	cups (465 g) pitted Kalamata olives
2	tablespoons olive oil
2	tablespoons nutritional yeast flakes
1	teaspoon mellow white miso
¼	cup (60 ml) vegetable broth, plus more for thinning
1	pound (455 g) angel hair pasta
6	cups (120 g) loosely packed baby arugula
	Sliced Kalamata olives, for serving
	Freshly ground black pepper

Serves 6 to 8

1. Make the grilled tofu: Slice the pressed tofu widthwise into eighths. In a 10-inch (25 cm) square baking dish, mix together the broth, olive oil, balsamic, tamari, and Italian seasoning. Place the tofu slabs in the marinade for about an hour, flipping once.

2. Lightly spray a grill pan with nonstick cooking spray and preheat over medium-high heat. Cook the tofu for about 3 minutes on each side, flipping once, until the tofu develops grill marks. Transfer to a plate and keep warm while you make the pasta.

3. Make the pasta: In a large pot, boil 6 quarts (5.7 L) of salted water for the pasta.

4. Meanwhile, make the tapenade: Pulse the garlic in a blender until well chopped. Add the olives, olive oil, nutritional yeast, miso, and vegetable broth and puree until the mixture is juicy but still has some texture. It shouldn't have whole chunks of olives, but it shouldn't be completely smooth. Add more broth to thin the tapenade as needed, scraping down the sides of the blender with a rubber spatula.

5. Cook the angel hair pasta according to package directions, usually 3 to 4 minutes.

6. Drain the pasta in a large colander. Put the arugula in the empty pasta pot, then immediately return the hot pasta to the pot. Toss with tongs to wilt the arugula.

7. Add the tapenade and toss to coat. Serve immediately, garnished with extra olives, lots of freshly ground black pepper, and the grilled tofu.

I Can Cook Vegan

Curry Udon with Broccoli and Avocado

Udon is a stick-to-your-ribs noodle. So plump and satisfying. Soaks up flavor really nicely, so I love to toss them in this gingery, coconut-y curry sauce and let it do its thing! If you can find already-cooked udon, that makes this recipe even easier.

Ingredients

Serves 4

8	ounces (225 g) dried udon noodles (choose the thick round ones)
6	cups (540 g) broccoli florets
2	tablespoons refined coconut oil
1	large red bell pepper, seeded and cut into ¼-inch-thick (6 mm) slices
2	teaspoons minced fresh ginger
3	cloves garlic, minced
	Big pinch red pepper flakes
1	cup (240 ml) vegetable broth
1	(15-ounce/430 g) can light coconut milk
1	tablespoon curry powder
1	tablespoon tamari
1	avocado, peeled, pitted, and diced
4	teaspoons toasted sesame seeds
	Chopped fresh cilantro, for serving

1. In a large pot, bring 4 quarts (3.8 L) of salted water to a boil. Boil the noodles according to package directions.

2. Preheat a large heavy-bottomed pan over medium heat. Sauté the broccoli in 1 tablespoon of the coconut oil and a pinch of salt until nicely seared, about 7 minutes. Transfer to a plate.

3. Sauté the red pepper slices in the pan with the remaining tablespoon coconut oil until seared, about 5 minutes. Add the ginger and garlic and sauté for about 1 minute, then mix in the red pepper flakes. Add the vegetable broth, coconut milk, curry powder, and tamari and bring to a boil.

4. Drain the noodles in a large colander. Add the noodles and reserved broccoli to the pan and mix to coat with the curry sauce. Serve in bowls topped with avocado, sesame seeds, and cilantro.

Spinach Manicotti

This manicotti has all the irresistible flavors that make for a stuff-your-face Sunday night dinner. Marinara, lots of garlic, and a creamy mozzy topping. Thaw the spinach at least 24 hours in advance and squeeze out excess moisture before using. To get this dish done as quickly as possible, boil the water first and make the ricotta while you're waiting. Have a sheet of parchment paper ready to rest the drained pasta on so it doesn't stick together after cooking. If you don't want to use Melty Mozzy (page 274) for whatever reason, sprinkle the stuffed pasta with breadcrumbs and drizzle with olive oil before baking. You will need a pastry bag and a large piping tip to neatly get the ricotta into the manicotti. However, if you don't have one (and want to get a little messy), use a teaspoon to spoon the ricotta into the pasta, then use your finger to push it all the way in.

For the ricotta

2   (14-ounce/400 g) blocks extra-firm tofu, drained
1   teaspoon salt
¼   cup (35 g) nutritional yeast flakes
¼   cup (60 ml) olive oil
3   tablespoons fresh lemon juice
1   (10-ounce/280 g) package frozen spinach, thawed (see headnote)

Everything else

8   ounces (225 g) manicotti
6   cups (1.4 L) marinara sauce, store-bought or homemade (page 278)
1   recipe Melty Mozzy (optional; see headnote)
    Freshly ground black pepper
½   cup (20 g) chopped fresh basil, for garnish

Serves 6 to 8

1.   Make the ricotta: Use your hands to mash the tofu into a ricotta-like consistency. You can't really overmash it, so just go until it's nice and mushy with a bit of curdlike texture left. Using a spoon or fork, mix in the salt, nutritional yeast, olive oil, and lemon juice. Mix in clumps of the spinach, tearing apart any big pieces, until well combined. Taste and adjust salt and seasoning.

2.   Place the ricotta in a piping bag fit with a wide tip, or a large freezer bag with a ½-inch (12 mm) hole cut out of one corner.

3.   In the meantime, boil the manicotti in a large pot of salted water according to package directions, being careful not to overcook it. Drain the pasta and, as soon as it's cool enough to touch, spread it out on the prepared piece of parchment to cool a bit more (see headnote).

4.   Preheat the oven to 375°F (195°C). Lightly spray a 9 by 13-inch (23 by 33 cm) casserole dish with nonstick cooking spray (or lightly grease it with a bit of olive oil). Coat the bottom of the pan with 3 cups (720 ml) of the marinara.

5.   Fill each manicotti with ricotta, usually a scant ¼ cup (60 g). Line the stuffed noodles up in the casserole dish so they are lightly touching. Top with the remaining 3 cups (720 ml) sauce, leaving the stuffed ends of the pasta exposed. Drizzle the Melty Mozzy over the top, if desired. Cover the casserole tightly with aluminum foil.

6.   Bake for 20 minutes. Remove the foil and bake for 10 minutes more. Let sit for about 10 minutes, then serve topped with fresh black pepper and basil.

I Can Cook Vegan

Lentil Walnut Bolognese

This is total Italian-night satisfaction. Thick noodles are tossed and folded in order to catch all the wonderfulness of a hearty, meaty marinara. The lentils are a perfect translation for ground meat; lightly mashed, they thicken the sauce and contribute a complex, naturally kind of beefy flavor. Add the nutty earthiness of chopped walnuts—and voilà!—ideal texture is achieved. Pappardelle is a wide noodle often served with Bolognese sauce that I actually have trouble finding in a vegan version, so I started using lasagna noodles instead and I love how they work! Especially the frilly-edge ones. The sauce clings to these noodles fabulously. But if you can find vegan pappardelle, go for it! Fettuccine is nice with this sauce as well.

Ingredients

Serves 6 to 8

1½ cups (300 g) cooked lentils, or 1 (15-ounce/430 g) can, drained and rinsed
2 tablespoons olive oil
2 ribs celery, finely chopped
1 medium yellow onion, thinly sliced
3 cloves garlic, minced
1 teaspoon dried thyme
1 teaspoon dried oregano
½ teaspoon red pepper flakes
   Freshly ground black pepper
1 (24-ounce/680 g) can crushed tomatoes with basil
1 teaspoon salt
12 ounces (340 g) lasagna noodles (see headnote)
1 cup (120 g) finely chopped walnuts
¼ cup (13 g) finely chopped fresh flat-leaf parsley, for garnish

1. In a large pot, bring 4 quarts (3.8 L) of salted water to a boil for the pasta.

2. In a wide, shallow bowl, mash the lentils with a fork until they're about half mashed, with some lentils still whole. Set aside.

3. Preheat a large sauté pan over medium heat. Sauté the celery and onion in the oil with a pinch of salt for about 5 minutes, until the onions are translucent. Add the garlic and sauté until fragrant, about 30 seconds. Mix in the thyme, oregano, red pepper flakes, and black pepper. Add the tomatoes and salt and stir everything together. Cover the pot, leaving a little gap for steam to escape, and cook for 15 minutes.

4. Break the lasagna noodles roughly in half. Add them to the pot of boiling water one by one to prevent them from sticking together. Use a pasta spoon to mix often until noodles are cooked according to package directions.

5. Add the mashed lentils and ½ cup (60 g) of the walnuts to the sauce (reserve the rest of the walnuts for garnish) and let cook uncovered for 5 minutes more.

6. Use the slotted pasta spoon to transfer the lasagna noodles into the Bolognese sauce. Toss well and cook for 3 minutes more, until the sauce has sunk into the noodles nicely. Serve, topped with the remaining ½ cup (60 g) walnuts and fresh parsley.

Penne Vodka

A staple in American Italian restaurants, and on my dinner table as well—who doesn't love creamy tomato sauce? There is no reason to deprive yourself of it because, OMG, cashew cream is indistinguishable from heavy cream here! This will be your go-to recipe for impressing dates or dinner party guests or even yourself when you just wanna whip something up for a Sunday night Netflix session. I love using coconut oil to sauté the onions because it resembles butter a little more than olive oil does. I realize that coconut oil is soooo not Italian, but just trust me. I also prefer to slice the garlic, rather than mince it, because it gets fabulously caramelized and creates garlic-bite flavor bombs. It's great topped with Eggplant Lardons (pictured; recipe on page 276), plus Seitan (page 280), or even some store-bought vegan chicken.

Ingredients

- 3 tablespoons refined coconut oil
- ¼ cup (35 g) thinly sliced garlic
- ½ cup (60 g) thinly sliced shallots
- 1 (25-ounce/710 g) can crushed tomatoes
- 1 teaspoon salt
- ½ teaspoon red pepper flakes
  Freshly ground black pepper
- ½ cup (120 ml) vodka
- 1 pound (455 g) penne
- ½ cup (60 g) whole unroasted cashews (if you don't own a high-speed blender, see page 24)
- ½ cup (120 ml) vegetable broth
- ½ cup (20 g) sliced fresh basil leaves

Serves 6

1. In a large pot, bring 4 quarts (3.8 L) of salted water to a boil for the pasta.

2. Preheat a large sauté pan over medium-low heat. Melt the coconut oil in the pan and immediately add the garlic, flipping it often until lightly browned on both sides, about 2 minutes. Add the shallots and a pinch of salt, turn the heat up to medium, then mix everything together and sauté until the shallots are translucent, about 3 minutes. Add the crushed tomatoes and scrape the bottom of the pan to make sure everything comes together. Add the salt, red pepper flakes, black pepper to taste, and the vodka. Bring to a steady simmer and allow the alcohol to cook out, 7 to 10 minutes.

3. Meanwhile, boil the penne according to package directions until al dente.

4. Place the cashews and vegetable broth in a high-speed blender and blend for about a minute or until completely smooth, using a rubber spatula to scrape down the sides every 20 seconds or so.

5. Add the cashew cream and half of the basil to the sauce (reserve the rest of the basil for garnish). Mix well.

6. Use a slotted pasta spoon or large wire skimmer to fish the pasta out of the water and add it to the sauce. Continue to simmer until the pasta is fully cooked and the sauce is clinging to the penne, 3 to 5 minutes. Serve topped with the reserved fresh basil and freshly ground black pepper.

I Can Cook Vegan

Shroom and White Bean Scampi

I grew up in a fishing community in Brooklyn with a large Italian American population, so you can bet I know my way around a shrimp scampi. It's got to be garlicky and lemony and fresh and absolutely gorgeous, too! "Scampi" isn't just a cute word, it's a crustacean, and shrimp is actually a substitute for scampi. Thus, shrooms replacing shrimp makes total sense! Especially when they're oyster mushrooms, which have a seafood-like quality. White beans add a little heartiness, making this the sort of pasta dish I would have no reservations serving to a few Sheepshead Bay fishermen. Beyond being a vehicle to prove that I can cook for fishermen, this dish is also wonderful for new cooks looking to try out some very easy methods that yield big flavors. Sautéing mushrooms releases their savory juices. You also reduce wine with lots of garlic, a method you will use again and again for a depth of flavor that tastes like you've been cooking all day. But, tee-hee, it's only been like 30 minutes. Definitely serve this to company!

Ingredients

Serves 6

1   pound (455 g) linguine
½   cup (60 g) thinly sliced shallots
2   tablespoons refined coconut oil
6   cloves garlic, minced
8   ounces (225 g) cremini mushrooms
8   ounces (225 g) oyster mushrooms
½   teaspoon red pepper flakes
    Freshly ground black pepper
1   teaspoon salt
1   cup (240 ml) dry white wine
1   cup (240 ml) vegetable broth, plus up to ½ cup (120 ml) more
1   (15-ounce/430 g) can white beans, drained and rinsed
2   tablespoons fresh lemon juice
¼   cup (13 g) chopped fresh flat-leaf parsley, plus more for garnish
    About 10 thin lemon slices

1. Bring 6 quarts (5.7 L) of salted water to a boil in a large pot. Boil the linguine according to package directions.

2. Meanwhile, preheat a large sauté pan over medium heat. Sauté the shallots in coconut oil with a pinch of salt, just until translucent, about 3 minutes. Add the garlic and sauté until fragrant, about a minute. Add the mushrooms, red pepper flakes, black pepper to taste, and the salt and sauté just until the juices are released, about 5 minutes. Pour in the wine, turn up the heat to medium-high, and use your spatula to scrape the bottom of the pan to get the good stuff. Let the wine boil and reduce for about 3 minutes.

3. Return the heat to medium and add the vegetable broth, beans, lemon juice, and parsley. Use a slotted pasta spoon or wire skimmer to transfer the pasta to the sauce and toss to coat. If the sauce seems dry, add up to ½ cup (120 ml) extra vegetable broth. Taste for salt and seasoning. Serve topped with fresh lemon slices and extra parsley.

Brussels Sprouts Pad Thai

Pad Thai is all about balance. Sweet, salty, spicy, tangy. So how do we get there? For the sweet, let's keep it simple, a little brown sugar. Tamari and miso team up for a one-two salty umami punch, as well as a little fermented flavor that you might find in traditional fish sauce. Red pepper flakes are probably not the spice you'll find in Thailand or in Thai restaurants, but they are so pantry-friendly and they get the job done! Now for the tangy . . . tamarind concentrate! It's got an ethereal flavor, sort of tart like a plum, but also a little tropical, and I just love to keep it around for occasions such as these. It's also nice and sticky, which is exactly what you want in pad Thai sauce. Brussels sprouts are a really welcome addition to this Thai standby. I first tried it this way in San Francisco in the 1990s. It's like you're wondering if pad Thai can get any better, and then suddenly there's roasty brussels, and holy-moly something already perfect is made even more so.

For the sauce

3 tablespoons tomato paste
⅓ cup (75 ml) tamari
⅓ cup (75 g) packed brown sugar
2 tablespoons tamarind concentrate
1 teaspoon red pepper flakes
3 tablespoons mellow white miso

For the noodles

8 ounces (225 g) pad Thai rice noodles
1 bunch scallions
3 tablespoons refined coconut oil
1 pound (455 g) brussels sprouts, trimmed and quartered (about 4 cups)
4 cloves garlic, minced
2 cups (40 g) loosely packed fresh cilantro leaves, lightly chopped
4 ounces (115 g) mung bean sprouts

For garnish

1 large carrot, cut into matchsticks
1 cup (150 g) roasted peanuts, finely chopped
Lime wedges

Recipe continues

Serves 6

1. Prepare the sauce: Mix all the ingredients together in a blender until smooth. You can also do this in a mixing bowl with a fork, but the blender is faster and smoother. A small blender, like a Magic Bullet, works really well. You can add up to ¼ cup (60 ml) of water to thin the sauce as needed.

2. Make the noodles: Bring a large pot of water to a boil. Cook the noodles according to package directions and be careful not to overcook. Drain in a colander and rinse with cold water to stop the cooking process.

3. Meanwhile, prepare the scallions by thinly slicing the white and light green parts about ⅛ inch (3 mm) thick. Slice the darker green parts into 1-inch (2.5 cm) pieces and keep separate.

4. Preheat a large sauté pan over medium-high heat. Melt 2 tablespoons of the coconut oil in the pan and sprinkle in a little salt. Add the brussels sprouts facedown in the pan and cook for about 6 minutes, turning after a few minutes, until browned on both sides and tender. Remove from the pan and set aside.

5. Now we'll cook the sauce in the same pan: Lower the heat to medium. Cook the garlic in the remaining 1 tablespoon oil very briefly, about 15 seconds. Add the dark green parts of the scallions and half of the cilantro and toss just to get it wilted. Now pour in about half the sauce and heat it through.

6. Add the noodles and toss to coat. Cook them through so that they're very hot. Add the cooked brussels and the mung bean sprouts and toss just to coat.

7. Serve immediately, topped with carrot matchsticks, peanuts, the white and light green parts of the scallions, and the remaining cilantro, with lime wedges alongside.

I Can Cook Vegan

But where does your pad Thai get its protein? This is a totally filling meal all on its own, but I do love to add and switch up proteins pretty often. A few options:

a. brown some tofu cubes in the pan before cooking the sauce, set aside and cook the sauce, then add back to the pan before throwing in the noodles;

b. do the same for small cubes of tempeh, browned for about 5 minutes in a few table-spoons of coconut oil;

c. drain a can of adzuki beans and add the beans to the pan before the sprouts;

d. this is my favorite!—sauté strips of yuba before cooking the sauce (pictured on page 49). Yuba mimics egg and tastes great. For yuba instructions, see page 190.

Chickpea Alfredo

You know that weeknight meal you're always in the mood for? This is it. A mix of cashews and almonds gives this alfredo a creaminess with a little texture to pull off a hard-cheese vibe. Chickpeas add a nice bite. I usually toss some of the chickpeas with an arugula or spinach salad dressed with lemon juice and olive oil to get my greens in, too.

Ingredients

Serves 6 to 8

1   pound (450 g) fettuccine
½   cup (60 g) whole unroasted
        cashews (if you don't
        own a high-speed
        blender, see page 24)
½   cup (55 g) slivered almonds
2   cloves garlic
1¼   cups (300 ml) vegetable broth
2   tablespoons mellow white miso
1   tablespoon fresh lemon juice
½   teaspoon salt
¼   cup (35 g) nutritional yeast flakes
1½   cups (240 g) cooked chickpeas,
        or 1 (15-ounce/430 g) can,
        drained and rinsed
¼   cup (13 g) minced fresh
        flat-leaf parsley
        Freshly ground black pepper

1.   Bring 6 quarts (5.7 L) of salted water to a boil in a large pot. Boil the pasta according to package directions.

2.   Meanwhile, in a high-speed blender, combine the cashews, almonds, garlic, vegetable broth, miso, lemon juice, salt, and nutritional yeast. Blend until relatively smooth, scraping down the sides with a rubber spatula once in a while to make sure you get everything.

3.   When the pasta is ready, drain it in a colander and immediately return it to the pot. Add the sauce, chickpeas, and parsley and toss to coat. Taste for salt and seasoning. Serve with black pepper over the top.

I Can Cook Vegan

Orzo with Asparagus and Edamame Ricotta

This dish is fresh, bright, garlicky, and lemony. The pasta itself is very simple, but the dollops of flavor-packed edamame ricotta give it that wow factor, and it's satisfying to mix it all up while you're eating. The plating makes it very fancy and special, adding that little photogenic touch that every vegan supper needs. Because if you didn't Instagram it, did you even have dinner? I love to work with orzo because it cooks so fast and has all the fun of risotto with none of the stirring. The ricotta is also a wonderful go-to for nut-free guests, so use it on salads and other pastas with aplomb.

For the edamame ricotta

- 2   cloves garlic, chopped
- 1   cup (30 g) packed fresh basil leaves
- 1   (14-ounce/400 g) package frozen shelled edamame, thawed
- ½   cup (120 ml) vegetable broth, plus more, if needed
- 2   tablespoons fresh lemon juice
- 1   teaspoon olive oil
- 1   teaspoon salt

For the pasta

- 1   pound (455 g) orzo
- 1   cup (115 g) thinly sliced shallots
- 3   tablespoons olive oil
- 6   cloves garlic, minced
- 1   pound (455 g) asparagus, tips trimmed, stems cut into ½-inch (12 mm) pieces
- 1   teaspoon salt
        Freshly ground black pepper
- 1   cup (240 ml) vegetable broth
- 2   tablespoons fresh lemon juice
        Fresh basil leaves, for garnish

Serves 6 to 8

1. Make the ricotta: Place the garlic and basil in a food processor and pulse a few times to get it chopped up. Add the edamame, vegetable broth, lemon juice, olive oil, and salt and blend until relatively smooth, scraping down the sides with a rubber spatula to make sure everything gets pureed. Add a little more broth if the ricotta seems too stiff. Set aside until ready to use.

2. Make the pasta: Bring 6 quarts (5.7 L) of salted water to a boil in a large pot. Boil the orzo according to package directions until al dente.

3. Preheat a large sauté pan over medium heat. Sauté the shallots in the oil with a pinch of salt, just until translucent, about 3 minutes. Add the garlic and sauté until fragrant, about 30 seconds. Add the asparagus, salt, and black pepper to taste and cook, stirring often, until softened, about 3 minutes. Add the vegetable broth and scrape the bottom of the pan to deglaze.

4. Add the pasta and lemon juice to the sauce and toss to coat. Serve in wide shallow bowls, if you've got them, with 3 dollops of ricotta on top of each serving and additional basil leaves.

Pesto Fusilli with Zucchini and Toasted Pine Nuts

Pesto is like the perfect denim jacket that goes with everything. But especially with pasta! Fusilli does a really great job of capturing sauce in all of its crevices, so I love it here. I use the spinach variety for some extra green, but obviously you can use regular fusilli. Or any other pasta, really. Zucchini cooks quickly in cast-iron and sears up beautifully. But use any summer squash that catches your eye at the farmers' market! For the pesto, let's be cheapskates and use walnuts instead of pine nuts. No one but a pine nut industry rep will be able to tell. Just sprinkle some on top and live like a king! I also sneak some arugula into the mix to save a little time and money, because who has the wherewithal to pick basil all day and night? I add some fresh cherry tomatoes to garnish because basil and tomatoes! The pop of color doesn't hurt, either.

For the pesto

3 cloves garlic
1 cup (95 g) walnut halves
3 cups (90 g) loosely packed fresh basil, plus extra for garnish
3 cups (120 g) loosely packed baby arugula
1½ teaspoons salt
¼ cup (35 g) nutritional yeast flakes
2 tablespoons fresh lemon juice
⅓ cup (75 ml) olive oil

For the pasta

1 pound (455 g) spinach fusilli
2 medium zucchini, sliced into rounds
1 tablespoon olive oil
Freshly ground black pepper
2 cups (290 g) halved cherry tomatoes
¼ cup (35 g) pine nuts, for garnish

Serves 6 to 8

1. Make the pesto: Place the garlic in a blender and pulse to chop it up. Add the walnuts and pulse into fine crumbs. Add the basil, arugula, salt, nutritional yeast, ½ cup (120 ml) water, and lemon juice and puree, leaving some texture. Stream in the olive oil and blend until well combined but not completely smooth. Taste for salt and adjust.

2. Make the pasta: Bring 6 quarts (5.7 L) of salted water to a boil in a large pot. Boil the fusilli according to package directions, usually 7 to 9 minutes.

3. Preheat a large heavy-bottomed pan over medium heat. Sauté the zucchini in the olive oil with a pinch of salt and plenty of black pepper until seared, about 7 minutes.

4. Drain the pasta in a large colander and immediately return it to the pot. Add the pesto and toss to heat through. Fold in the zucchini. Serve immediately, garnished with cherry tomatoes, pine nuts, and some extra black pepper.

I Can Cook Vegan

Chapter

Salads
Big
&
Small

Mission: Learn to combine flavor and texture—crunchy, fresh, crispy ISO smoky, tangy, earthy, sweet. You are the matchmaker, ready to bring them all together in perfect harmony! I also predict you'll have some good times at the farmers' market.

Salad is the purest expression of one's appetite. They're crafted often by instinct: What are you craving? What do you have around? In our modern world, the line between salad and main event have blurred. I'm not about to tell you how to make a side salad (wait, yes, I will: lettuces, cucumbers, tomatoes, and sprouts). Instead, here are more filling salads, which can be full-on lunches or dinners. Salads that will fill you up with amazing, healthy things (yes, potatoes are healthy) and never leave you wanting for anything. Except more salad.

Equipment must-haves

Tongs
Large mixing bowl
Resealable bags to
   keep produce fresh
Squeeze bottles
Kitchen shears
Large-ass colander
Mug and fork

Greens I buy all the time

Baby arugula
Mixed greens
Baby kale
Radicchio
Romaine hearts
Lacinato kale

Don't be afraid to grab a package of prepped kale or arugula. The taste is just as good, the greens are washed and trimmed, and sometimes that convenience is the only thing stopping us from ordering in. Just be sure to recycle your plastics, okay?

Salads Big & Small

Kale Caesar Salad with Roasted Brussels Sprouts

Caesar is the mother of all salads, vegan or not. But especially vegan! Who can deny a briny, lemony, creamy, garlicky dressing? I think the reason that kale Caesars in particular are so popular (besides the fact that the name sounds like "hail, Caesar," I suppose) is that the acidic dressing really breaks down the kale's toughness, revealing its true, velvety nature. It still retains its crunch and heartiness but after the massage it's, well, relaxed a bit! This dressing uses nori as a seasoning, adding that ocean flavor to the mix. I love roasted brussels sprouts instead of croutons, for their toasty crunch. If you'd like to add protein, toss in some chickpeas or top with Tempeh Bacon (page 68), Noochy Baked Tofu (page 281), or Grilled Tofu (page 36). Avocado, of course, never hurts, either. If you want to add croutons, see the recipe on page 281.

For the brussels sprouts

Serves 4 to 6

1   pound (455 g) brussels sprouts, quartered
2   tablespoons olive oil
½   teaspoon salt

For the dressing

3   cloves garlic
1   cup (120 g) whole unroasted cashews (if you don't own a high-speed blender, see page 24)
½   sheet nori, torn into pieces
¼   cup (35 g) nutritional yeast flakes
¼   cup (60 ml) fresh lemon juice
1   teaspoon whole-grain Dijon mustard
¾   teaspoon salt
     Several dashes freshly ground black pepper

1   pound (455 g) lacinato kale, tough stems removed, leaves torn into 2-inch (5 cm) pieces
     Roasted sunflower seeds, for garnish (optional)
     Freshly ground black pepper
     Lemon slices, for squeezing (optional)

1. Make the brussels sprouts: Preheat the oven to 425°F (220°C). Line a large baking sheet with parchment paper and set aside.

2. Toss the brussels sprouts with the olive oil and salt. Bake for 15 minutes, until lightly browned. No need to flip them, just let 'em roast.

3. Make the dressing: Place the garlic cloves in a high-speed blender and pulse to chop them up. Add the cashews, nori, nutritional yeast, ¾ cup (180 ml) water, lemon juice, mustard, salt, and pepper and and blend until completely smooth, about a minute, scraping down the sides with a rubber spatula every now and again.

4. Pour about three-quarters of the dressing into a large mixing bowl. Add the kale and massage it into the dressing with your hands for about a minute. Don't be afraid to really get in there like you're kneading dough.

5. Top with the roasted brussels sprouts and drizzle on more dressing. Finish with roasted sunflower seeds, if desired, and a little extra black pepper, and serve with lemon slices, if using!

Taco Salad Chorizo

Maybe you'd feel indulgent eating nachos any old night of the week, but this taco salad is a clever way to get your nachos and your veggies in. It is loaded with flavor from the walnut chorizo, which is a simple mix of chopped-up sun-dried tomatoes and walnuts. My friend Voni came up with this fabulous, crumbly taco meat, and I've been using it on everything! You might find yourself tossing the chorizo into tacos (obviously), on scrambles, over baked potatoes, or simply served alongside guac and chips. I use a food processor to get the job done quickly, but you can finely chop all the ingredients, as well—it will just take a bit longer.

For the chorizo

2	cloves garlic
2	cups (200 g) walnuts
½	cup (55 g) roughly chopped yellow onion
4	sun-dried tomatoes in oil (about ¼ cup/30 g, including oil)
1	tablespoon apple cider vinegar
2	teaspoons smoked paprika
1	teaspoon ground cumin
⅛	teaspoon cayenne
½	teaspoon salt

For the pico de gallo

1	cup (180 g) small-diced tomato
⅓	cup (40 g) finely chopped red onion
1	jalapeño, seeded and finely diced
½	cup (20 g) finely chopped fresh cilantro
2	tablespoons fresh lime juice
¼	teaspoon salt

For the salad

8	cups (455 g) chopped romaine
	Lime for squeezing (about 4 tablespoons juice)
	Flaky sea salt, such as Maldon brand
8	cups (500 g) tortilla chips
2	avocados, halved and sliced
1	cup (235 g) unsweetened plain coconut yogurt, stirred well

Serves 4 to 6

1. Make the chorizo: Preheat the oven to 350°F (175°C). Line a large baking sheet with parchment paper and set aside.

2. In a food processor fit with a metal blade, pulse the garlic until it's chopped. Add the walnuts and pulse to coarse crumbs. Add the onion and pulse again into pea-size pieces. Add the sun-dried tomatoes and their oil, apple cider vinegar, smoked paprika, cumin, cayenne, and salt. Pulse until all the ingredients are incorporated and the mixture resembles crumbled meat. You don't want to puree it, but don't leave large chunks of anything, either. Pieces should be no larger than, let's say, a pea.

3. Spread the chorizo mixture onto the prepared baking sheet and bake for 10 minutes.

Remove and keep warm (wrapping aluminum foil over the pan will work).

4. Make the pico: Mix all the ingredients (tomato, red onion, jalapeño, cilantro, lime juice, and salt) together in a mixing bowl. You can actually do this while the chorizo is baking.

5. Assemble each salad by spreading the romaine out on a plate. Drizzle with fresh lime juice and sprinkle with salt. Top with a layer of tortilla chips. Spoon warm chorizo over the chips and top with spoonfuls of pico de gallo. Add avocado slices to the center. Drizzle with coconut yogurt and serve.

I Can Cook Vegan

Warm German Potato Salad with Tempeh Bacon

I love a creamy, mustardy potato salad with loads of crunch. You don't need much more than that to elevate perfectly boiled potatoes. And, yes, there is such a thing as perfectly boiled potatoes. The secret isn't really a secret, it's simply small red potatoes. They have a delicate skin and are easy to prep since they're already tiny: just slice them in half! The tempeh bacon is a nod to German potato salad, which is served hot, but you can serve this warm or cold. To make it warm, simply mix the hot cooked potatoes with the dressing and serve immediately. Placing the potatoes in cold water before bringing them to a boil is the best way to make sure your potatoes don't overcook. Once the water is boiling, bring the heat down to simmer. Test after 10 minutes to see if the potatoes are fork tender. They will continue to cook a little bit as they cool.

For the tempeh bacon

2	tablespoons pure maple syrup
2	tablespoons tamari
2	tablespoons olive oil
2	tablespoons smoked paprika
8	ounces (225 g) tempeh, cut widthwise into ¼-inch (6 mm) slices

For the potato salad

1½	pounds (680 g) baby red potatoes, sliced in half or into 1-inch (2.5 cm) pieces
⅓	cup (75 ml) vegan mayo, store-bought or homemade (page 277)
⅓	cup (75 ml) Dijon mustard
1	tablespoon red wine vinegar
½	teaspoon salt
	Freshly ground black pepper
2	ribs celery, thinly sliced
6	cups (330 g) loosely packed mixed field greens
3	tablespoons chopped fresh flat-leaf parsley

Serves 4 to 6

1. Make the tempeh bacon: In a wide shallow bowl, whisk together the maple syrup, tamari, olive oil, 2 tablespoons water, and smoked paprika. Add the tempeh slices and marinate them for at least 20 minutes and up to an hour.

2. Make the potato salad: Place the potatoes in a 4-quart (3.8 L) pot and submerge them with salted water. Cover the pot and bring water to a boil. Lower the heat to a simmer and cook for about 10 more minutes, until the potatoes are easily pierced with a fork. Drain in a colander and set aside.

3. When the tempeh is marinated, preheat a large nonstick pan (preferably cast-iron) over medium heat. Spray the pan with a little nonstick cooking spray. Put the tempeh in the pan in a single layer, reserving the marinade. Pan-fry for about 10 minutes, until the tempeh is slightly blackened in some spots, flipping it occasionally with a thin metal spatula and adding splashes of marinade as you cook. Once ready, transfer to a plate and cover with aluminum foil to keep warm.

4. In a large mixing bowl, vigorously stir together the mayo, mustard, vinegar, salt, and pepper. Stir in the celery and then fold in the warm potatoes. Taste for salt and seasoning. Gently fold in the greens. Serve topped with the tempeh bacon and garnished with parsley.

Warm Oyster Mushroom Salad with Quinoa and Baby Greens

Beautiful mushrooms don't require much work to turn them into an exquisite meal. In fact, the opposite is true: The less you do to them, the better and more succulent they taste. Olive oil, salt, pepper, and a nice hot grill are everything! When you throw the salad together, the mushrooms wilt the greens a bit and create something fancy all on their own. Choose hearty baby greens if you can find them, like baby chard and kale. They hold up really nicely.

For the dressing

¼   cup (35 g) roughly chopped garlic
4   tablespoons (60 ml) olive oil
½   cup (120 ml) vegan mayo, store-bought or homemade (page 277)

For the salad

8   ounces (225 g) oyster mushrooms, stems trimmed
½   teaspoon salt
     Freshly ground black pepper
1   cup (200 g) cooked quinoa
6   ounces (170 g) mixed baby greens

Serves 4 to 6

1. To make the dressing, preheat a small pan over very low heat. Add the garlic and drizzle in 1 tablespoon of the olive oil. Cook for 2 minutes or so until lightly browned, stirring constantly. Immediately transfer to a small blender. Add the mayo and 2 tablespoons of water and blend until completely smooth. Depending on the thickness of the mayo, you may need to add more water. Taste for salt and set aside until ready to use.

2. Preheat a grill pan over medium heat. In a large mixing bowl, combine the mushrooms, remaining 3 tablespoons olive oil, salt, and pepper to taste and toss to coat completely. (You'll use this bowl again, so no need to clean it.) Grill the mushrooms on each side, pressing down lightly with a spatula, for about 3 minutes, or until dark grill marks appear and the mushrooms are soft.

3. Transfer the dressing to the large mixing bowl you used for the mushrooms. Use a rubber spatula to scrape the blender, making sure you get everything. Add the quinoa and greens and toss to coat completely.

4. Use tongs to transfer the dressed quinoa and greens to plates. Top with the grilled mushrooms and a little more freshly ground black pepper.

Buffalo Cauliflower Ranch Salad

If I go out to a restaurant that has both a ranch salad AND a buffalo anything on the menu, you can guarantee that I'm going to get my buffalo mixed up with the ranch and my ranch mixed up with the buffalo. So here is one of my favorite combos in one convenient recipe! I add a little quinoa for crunch and protein. The buffalo cauliflower is baked so that you can maintain your dignity and not have to break out a deep-fryer for a salad (not that I would judge). I prefer cucumbers to celery with my buffalo sauce, but if you're a "celery-or-bust" type, then go ahead and swap out the cukes for celery, or just use celery as a garnish. This recipe gets a little involved and may seem like it has a million steps, but that's because it's like a recipe within a recipe within a recipe. Just remember, you are learning lessons that will last you a lifetime! Like how to batter and bread things, and also how to bake said battered things instead of frying them. You also can just go ahead and serve the cauliflower with ranch dressing as its own little appetizer, or throw it on top of mac and cheese, or just make a big bowl of it and eat it in front of the TV or fireplace. And the ranch dressing is a treasure on its own! So make a triple batch and keep it on hand for any time a bag of baby rainbow carrots is calling out to be dipped.

For the ranch dressing

- ¼ cup (60 ml) vegan mayo, store-bought or homemade (page 277)
- ¼ cup (60 ml) unsweetened unflavored almond milk
- 2 tablespoons white vinegar
- ½ teaspoon garlic powder
- 1 teaspoon onion powder
- 1 teaspoon nutritional yeast flakes
- ⅛ teaspoon salt
- 3 tablespoons chopped fresh dill

For the buffalo cauliflower

- ½ cup plus 2 tablespoons (75 g) all-purpose flour
- 2 tablespoons cornstarch
- 1 cup (240 ml) cold water
- 1½ cups (150 g) breadcrumbs
- 1½ teaspoons rosemary, crushed between your fingers
- 1 teaspoon salt
- 3 tablespoons olive oil
- 1 large head cauliflower, cut into large (2-inch/5 cm) florets
- ¾ cup (180 ml) buffalo hot sauce (like Frank's RedHot)
- 2 tablespoons refined coconut oil, melted

For the salad

- 3 romaine hearts, chopped into 2-inch (5 cm) pieces
- 1 cup (200 g) cooked, cooled quinoa
- 1 cup (105 g) cucumber half-moon slices
- 1 cup (145 g) halved cherry tomatoes
- ½ cup (15 g) fresh dill sprigs, for garnish

Recipe continues

I Can Cook Vegan

Serves 4 to 6

1. Make the dressing: Mix all the ingredients in a mug. Use a fork and stir until well combined. Set aside.

2. Make the buffalo cauliflower: Preheat the oven to 450°F (230°C). Line a large rimmed baking sheet with parchment paper, spray it with nonstick cooking spray, and set aside.

3. You'll need a large bowl for the batter and a big rimmed plate for breading. Put the flour and cornstarch in the bowl. Add about half of the water and stir vigorously with a fork to dissolve. Add the rest of the water, and stir to incorporate. To prepare the breading, mix together the breadcrumbs, rosemary, and salt on the plate. Drizzle in the olive oil and use your fingertips to mix it up well.

4. Now pull together an assembly line to dip the cauli. From left to right, set out the cauliflower, the batter, the breadcrumb mixture, and lastly the baking sheet. Working one at a time, dip each cauliflower floret into the batter, letting the excess drip off. Transfer to the bowl of breadcrumbs and, using the other (dry) hand, toss to coat completely, pressing the breadcrumbs into the crevices of the floret as you go. Transfer each coated cauliflower to the prepared baking sheet to create a single layer.

5. Bake the cauliflower for 10 minutes. Flip and bake for another 5 to 7 minutes. The florets should be crisp and varying shades of brown. Taste one to check for doneness; it should be tender with some bite.

6. While the cauliflower is roasting, mix together the hot sauce and melted coconut oil in a bowl and set aside.

7. When you're ready to serve, pour the dressing into a large mixing bowl. Add the romaine, quinoa, cucumbers, and cherry tomatoes and toss to coat. Transfer to individual plates. While the cauliflower is still warm, use a large spoon to dip each floret in the hot sauce, drip off the excess, and arrange on top of the salad greens. Serve immediately.

I Can Cook Vegan

I say buffalo sauce
like Frank's RedHot,
but what I mean
is … Frank's RedHot.
Honestly, nothing else
will do to achieve that
real buffalo taste.
They don't pay me to
say this, but I wish
they would!

Curried Kale and Quinoa Salad with Almonds and Raisins

This nutty kale salad has bursts of sweet raisins and plenty of crunch from toasted almonds and quinoa. The dressing is a luxurious curried almond butter concoction that really packs a punch. Once again, you get tons of flavor and a more lush texture from your kale by massaging it with citrus, oil, and salt. After that, everything else is gravy. I mean dressing! If you want to bulk this salad up, no one would be mad if you added chickpeas and/or avocado.

For the dressing

½ cup (135 g) almond butter, at room temperature
2 teaspoons curry powder
3 tablespoons rice vinegar
2 teaspoons agave
1 tablespoon Sriracha sauce
½ teaspoon salt

For the salad

1 cup (95 g) sliced almonds
6 cups (390 g) roughly torn loosely packed curly kale, rough stems discarded
2 tablespoons fresh lime juice
2 tablespoons olive oil
½ teaspoon coarse salt
1 cup (200 g) cooked quinoa
1 cup (145 g) raisins
Flaky sea salt, such as Maldon brand
½ cup (20 g) fresh cilantro leaves, for garnish

Serves 4 to 6

1. Make the dressing: In a blender, combine the almond butter, curry powder, rice vinegar, agave, Sriracha, salt, and ¼ cup (60 ml) water and blend until completely smooth. Add more water, a little at a time, to thin the dressing, if necessary.

2. Make the salad: Preheat a large skillet over medium-low heat. Once hot, spread out the almonds in a single layer and toast them, flipping every 30 seconds or so, until slightly golden. Transfer to a bowl and set aside.

3. Place the kale in a very large mixing bowl. Drizzle in the lime juice and olive oil and sprinkle on the salt. Rub the kale with your fingers for a minute or so, rubbing the salt and oil onto all of the leaves. Toss in the quinoa and mix well.

4. To assemble the salad, divide the kale among bowls and drizzle with the dressing. Top with the reserved almonds and the raisins and finish with pinches of flaky sea salt and the fresh cilantro.

Caprese with Almond Ricotta

First, let's get this pronunciation down, because you're saying it wrong: "CA-PRAY-ZAY." Great. Moving on, I must tell you that the tomatoes are the most important element. So, if it's just not the right season and you can't find big, juicy, just-off-the-vine 'matos, then don't bother. Now that those things are cleared up, let's get CA-RAY-ZAY. Fresh basil, sweet balsamic reduction, olive oil, and salt make for the simplest but most sublime summer salad. Traditionally, mozzarella is the cheese of choice, but ricotta is not unheard of and almond ricotta is a nice introduction to vegan cheese making. Use the fruitiest, fanciest olive oil—the "good stuff"—for this recipe.

For the balsamic reduction

2   cups (480 ml) balsamic vinegar

For the ricotta

1½   cups (145 g) slivered almonds
½   cup (120 ml) warm water
2   tablespoons olive oil
2   tablespoons nutritional
        yeast flakes
2   tablespoons fresh lemon juice
½   teaspoon salt

For the salad

4   large vine-ripened tomatoes,
        sliced ¼ inch (6 mm) thick
    Olive oil, for drizzling
    Flaky or coarse sea salt,
        such as Maldon brand
    Freshly ground black pepper
2   cups (60 g) loosely packed
        fresh basil leaves

Serves 4

1. Make the balsamic reduction: Pour the vinegar into a small pot over medium-high heat and bring to a boil. Lower the heat and simmer the balsamic for about 20 minutes, stirring every few minutes with a fork, until a sticky, syrupy consistency develops and the balsamic is reduced by about half. Err on the side of caution and don't set the heat too high or let the vinegar come to a boil, or the end result might be too stiff. Once the reduction is thick and syrupy, transfer to a small sealable container. Store at room temperature.

2. Make the ricotta: Place the almonds in a blender or food processor and pulse into crumbs. Add the water, olive oil, nutritional yeast, lemon juice, and salt and blend until a thick and pasty, ricotta-like texture is achieved. Use a rubber spatula to transfer to an airtight container and chill until ready to use.

3. To assemble the salad, use a spoon to drizzle the balsamic reduction on each plate in a circular motion. Place tomatoes on each plate (as pictured on opposite page), on top of the balsamic. Dollop the almond ricotta on the tomatoes, drizzle with olive oil, and sprinkle with flaky salt. Grind some fresh black pepper over everything. Top each serving with basil leaves and serve immediately.

I Can Cook Vegan

Minty Tabbouleh with Baked Falafel and Tzatziki

I love a good falafel salad! This one is definitely not a throw-together salad, it's more of a feast. The falafel are perfectly seasoned—bright green inside from the fresh herbs, not those sad brown balls you see at the food court. And the tabbouleh is also loaded with fresh herbs and bright flavor: fresh lemon, refreshing cucumber, and even more chickpeas for good measure. Oh my yum. So yeah, this is a three-part recipe that you can make and serve all together, but the components are also great on their own! Who doesn't need a baked falafel? And a tabbouleh that actually fills you up? Not to mention a tzatziki that can turn anything into a Mediterranean feast!

For the falafel

1 (29-ounce/830 g) can chickpeas, drained and rinsed, or 3 cups (475 g) cooked chickpeas
3 cloves garlic, minced
¼ cup (30 g) chopped yellow onion
¼ cup (13 g) chopped fresh flat-leaf parsley
¼ cup (10 g) chopped fresh cilantro
½ teaspoon cayenne
1½ teaspoons ground cumin
3 tablespoons olive oil
¼ cup (30 g) all-purpose flour, plus 1 tablespoon, if needed
½ teaspoon baking powder
½ teaspoon salt
   Freshly ground black pepper

For the tabbouleh

1 cup (140 g) bulghur wheat
3 tablespoons olive oil
1½ cups (360 ml) boiling water
1 teaspoon salt
3 tablespoons fresh lemon juice
1 cup (50 g) finely chopped fresh mint leaves
1 cup (50 g) finely chopped fresh flat-leaf parsley
1 cup (180 g) small-diced tomato
1 cup (110 g) small-diced English (hothouse) cucumber
1 (15-ounce/430 g) can chickpeas, drained and rinsed, or about 1½ cups (240 g) cooked chickpeas

For the tzatziki

2 cloves garlic
1 (8-ounce/225 g) container unsweetened plain coconut yogurt
2 tablespoons fresh lemon juice
2 tablespoons olive oil
½ teaspoon salt
1 cup (110 g) roughly chopped cucumber
¼ cup (13 g) chopped fresh dill

For serving

6 cups (330 g) loosely packed mixed baby greens
   Chopped fresh flat-leaf parsley
   Toasted pine nuts
   Freshly ground black pepper

Recipe continues

I Can Cook Vegan

Serves 6 to 8

1.   Make the falafel: Preheat the oven to 400°F (205°C). Line a large baking sheet with parchment paper, spray it with nonstick cooking spray, and set aside.

2.   Pulse the chickpeas in a food processor, or finely mash them with a potato masher. Transfer the mashed chickpeas to a mixing bowl and add the garlic, onion, parsley, cilantro, cayenne, cumin, and olive oil and mix really really well. Add the flour, baking powder, salt, and pepper to taste and use your hands to mix well. The falafel mixture should be firm enough to shape into balls. If it seems too mushy, mix in an additional tablespoon of flour.

3.   Form the mixture into walnut-size balls, then flatten them a bit to form patties. Place the patties in equally spaced rows on the prepared baking sheet and give them a light spray of nonstick cooking spray.

4.   Bake for 16 to 18 minutes, until the falafel are browned on the underside. Remove from the oven, flip the falafel patties over, and bake for 8 to 10 minutes more.

5.   Make the tzatziki: In a blender, pulse the garlic to chop it. Add the yogurt, lemon juice, olive oil, and salt and blend until smooth. Add the cucumber and dill and pulse until the cucumber is chopped into tiny pieces. If the dressing needs further seasoning, transfer it to a mixing bowl and stir it in so that you don't puree this into a smoothie.

6.   Make the tabbouleh: Place the bulghur in a medium mixing bowl. Drizzle with 1 tablespoon of the olive oil and sprinkle on the salt. Measure out 1 cup (240 ml) of the boiling water and pour it over the bulghur. Immediately cover the bowl with a plate and steam the grains for 15 minutes or so, until the water is absorbed. Fluff with a fork and let cool completely.

7.   Transfer the cooled bulghur to a large mixing bowl. Drizzle in the remaining 2 tablespoons olive oil, the salt, lemon juice, mint, parsley, tomato, cucumber, and chickpeas. Toss well with your hands to completely coat; this usually takes at least 2 minutes. Taste for salt and seasoning.

8.   To assemble the salad, place the greens on a large plate or platter, top with tabbouleh, and then place the falafel on top. Drizzle on the dressing and sprinkle with parsley, pine nuts, and freshly ground pepper.

I Can Cook Vegan

Want to make a falafel sandwich instead? Great, because that will be a whole lot easier. You'll need to chop up tomato, red onion, and cucumber and toss them with red wine vinegar and a bit of salt, akin to a salsa. In a blender, thin out some tahini with water, a splash of fresh lemon, and a lil salt.

Now get a few pitas and split them in half. Stuff with the lettuce and the salsa, drizzle with tahini. Add three falafel balls and drizzle those with tahini, too. I also like to add some sour pickles. And if you're feeling like I'm feeling, some fresh cilantro, too.

Sweet Potato and Blood Orange Salad with Mustard Vinaigrette

Citrus and sweet potato shine together here, creating a wintery salad that's just as eye-popping as it is mouthwatering. A creamy, tangy mustard vinaigrette brings it all together, and fresh mint takes it to the next level. To make this salad a meal, top it with Tempeh Bacon (page 68) or grilled seitan. If you can't find blood oranges, that's too bad, but Valencia oranges would be just fine, too! Or even ruby red grapefruit.

For the salad

Serves 4

1   pound (455 g) sweet potatoes, peeled and cut into 1-inch (2.5 cm) chunks
2   tablespoons olive oil
½   teaspoon salt

For the dressing

¼   cup (60 ml) Dijon mustard
¼   cup (60 ml) vegan mayo, store-bought or homemade (page 277)
1   clove garlic, minced
1   tablespoon white wine vinegar
8   cups (440 g) loosely packed field greens or baby greens
3   blood oranges, cut into segments
1   red onion, thinly sliced
2   tablespoons toasted pine nuts
¼   cup (13 g) chopped fresh mint leaves

1.   Preheat the oven to 425°F (220°C). Line a large baking sheet with parchment paper. Toss the sweet potatoes with the oil and salt and arrange them in a single layer on the parchment. Bake for 20 to 25 minutes, tossing once, until softened. Set aside.

2.   In a mug, mix together the mustard, mayo, garlic, vinegar, and a big pinch of salt. Stir with a fork until nice and creamy.

3.   To assemble, place the greens in a medium-size bowl. Top with the sweet potatoes, orange segments, and red onion. Drizzle with the dressing and sprinkle with the pine nuts and mint.

Soba Noodle Salad with Edamame and Kimchi

This is kind of a semi-homemade salad for cheaters, but you need a few of those in your life! It's got all the Korean flavors I absolutely love: pungent, tangy spice from the kimchi, warm and toasty sesame. Kimchi really can do no wrong and generously flavors the noodles. I use store-bought baked tofu because why not? But you can make your own if you choose (page 281). If you can't find packaged cooked edamame, use frozen edamame, thawed to room temperature.

Ingredients

Serves 4

8	ounces (225 g) buckwheat soba noodles
1	tablespoon soy sauce
1	tablespoon toasted sesame oil
1½	cups (240 g) shelled edamame
1	(6-ounce/170 g) package baked tofu, sliced into strips
2	cups (300 g) store-bought kimchi
2	tablespoons toasted sesame seeds
½	cup (50 g) thinly sliced scallions (white and light green parts only), for garnish

1. Bring a large pot of water to a rolling boil. Add the soba noodles and boil them according to the package directions, being careful not to overcook. Once the noodles are tender, transfer them to a colander to drain and run under cold water to cool completely. Set aside.

2. In a large bowl, whisk together the soy sauce and sesame oil. Add the noodles, edamame, tofu, kimchi, and sesame seeds. Using your hands, toss to combine, making sure not to break up the tofu. Garnish with the scallions and serve!

Chapter

3

Sand-
wiches

Mission: These recipes will get us acquainted, or reacquainted, with some of the most beloved sandwiches in the world. Better still, they will give you an understanding of how to translate some well-known handheld comfort foods into their beautiful vegan versions.

Making sandwiches is where I started my cooking journey. By first grade I could throw together something with cold cuts and mayonnaise. Then came tuna fish and egg salad sandwiches. And at some point between second grade and voting in my first election I made my way to grilled cheese. While no one is giving away any Michelin stars for these accomplishments, they're definitely the start of cooking! So consider these sandwiches a fun little gateway to more serious cooking. You can get out the cutting board and play with combinations. Figure out your taste preferences—mayo or mustard? Red onion or nah? And in the end, you get a meal out of the deal! This chapter isn't just about stuff between bread, either; it encompasses anything we eat with our hands, from tacos to pizza. So all the major food groups.

Sandwiches

Tempeh Beet Reuben

I have to issue a few warnings about this sandwich: You will end up covered in orange dressing. Some sauerkraut will fall on your cat's head. And if those things don't happen, you're eating it wrong. Tangy tempeh and thinly sliced beets lend a corned-beefy Eastern European flair to this sandwich. With the caraway rye, sauerkraut, and Russian dressing, it definitely hits all the right notes! If you'd like to take it a step further, homemade Swizz Cheese (page 276) drives the point home, but in a pinch some sliced avocado works really well instead—that's how we ate Reubens in the 1990s and we loved it.

Ingredients

½ cup (120 ml) vegetable broth
4 tablespoons (60 ml) olive oil
¼ cup (60 ml) fresh lemon juice
2 tablespoons tamari
  Freshly ground black pepper
1 pound (455 g) tempeh, cut into 4 equal pieces, then cut across like a clamshell so that you have 8 thin pieces
1 tennis ball-size beet, sliced as thin as you can get it
⅓ cup (75 ml) vegan mayo, store-bought or homemade (page 277)
2 tablespoons ketchup
1 tablespoon onion powder
¼ cup (40 g) finely chopped dill pickles
8 large slices caraway rye bread
1½ cups (375 g) sauerkraut, drained (reserve liquid if making Swizz Cheese)
  Dill pickle slices on toothpicks, for garnish

Makes 4 sandwiches

1. In a large mixing bowl, whisk together the vegetable broth, 2 tablespoons of the olive oil, lemon juice, tamari, and black pepper to taste. Add the tempeh and beet slices and marinate for at least an hour, turning occasionally.

2. Meanwhile, make the dressing: In a mug, mix the mayonnaise, ketchup, onion powder, and chopped dill pickles. Set aside.

3. When you're ready to cook the filling, preheat a cast-iron skillet over medium heat. Add the remaining 2 tablespoons oil to the pan. Using a slotted spoon, remove the tempeh and beets from the marinade, shake off excess liquid, and place them in the hot pan in a single layer. (A little overlapping is okay.) Cook for about 10 minutes, using a thin metal spatula to turn them often. When the beets are softened and the tempeh is browned, it's ready!

4. Toast the bread and spread the dressing on all the slices. Evenly divide the tempeh and beets among 4 slices of toast. If desired, pour a few tablespoons of warm Swizz Cheese on top of each pile of tempeh and beets. Add the sauerkraut, dividing it evenly among the Reubens, then close the sandwiches. Spike with dill pickle toothpicks and serve.

I Can Cook Vegan

Grilled Curry Tofu Banh Mi

"Banh mi" has become a verb in my household; I'll banh mi anything simply by putting some pickles, mayo, and cilantro on it! From burgers to Tofurky sandwiches, the flavor combo really can't steer you wrong. But how about we banh mi an actual banh mi? The only trick here is that we're using curried tofu. The hint of star anise in the marinade gives the tofu even more Vietnamese flavor and the smokiness from the grill completes me. This sandwich is easy to put together; just marinate the tofu while the pickles are working and it practically makes itself.

For the pickles

½ cup (60 g) shredded radish
½ cup (55 g) shredded carrots
2 tablespoons rice vinegar
2 teaspoons agave
   Pinch salt

For the tofu

1 cup (240 ml) vegetable broth
2 tablespoons olive oil
2 tablespoons tamari
1 tablespoon curry powder
3 star anise pods
1 (8-ounce/225 g) block extra-firm tofu, drained and pressed, sliced into 8 slabs

For the spicy mayo

¼ cup (60 ml) vegan mayo, store-bought or homemade (page 277)
2 teaspoons rice vinegar
2 teaspoons Sriracha sauce

For the sandwiches

2 French baguettes (6 to 8 inches/15 to 20 cm each), split in half
1 large handful fresh cilantro, leaves and stems

Makes 4 sandwiches

1. Make the pickles: Toss all the ingredients together in a mixing bowl and let sit for a few minutes, until ready to serve. Give everything a stir every now and again when you think of it.

2. Make the tofu: In a large mixing bowl, mix together the vegetable broth, olive oil, tamari, curry powder, and star anise. Add the tofu slabs and toss to coat. Let marinate for an hour or so, turning once.

3. Preheat a cast-iron grill pan over medium heat. Coat the bottom with nonstick cooking spray. Cook the tofu for 3 to 5 minutes on each side, or until dark grill marks appear. Use a thin metal spatula to get under the tofu when you flip it.

4. Make the spicy mayo: In a mug, mix together all the ingredients.

5. Spread both halves of the baguettes with the mayo. Add the tofu, followed by the pickles, and finally the cilantro. Close the baguettes, cut them in half, and have at it!

Classic Lentil Burger

The veggie burger is never given enough credit, but are you ever NOT in the mood for one? You absolutely need a basic veggie burger recipe in your life! One that's this side of meaty, but not quite imitation meat. One that has a few veggies, but there's not broccoli and carrots sticking out of it. As the title implies, these are classic. A little smoky, lots of texture, with appealing burger color from the lentils. And yes, burger color is important! The mixture needs to chill for 30 minutes for the absolute best results, so maybe make it a day ahead and have dinner on the table in no time the next day. Serve on burger buns (obvs) with all the usual fixings!

Ingredients

1   small yellow onion, chopped into medium dice
2   tablespoons olive oil
8   ounces (225 g) cremini mushrooms, roughly chopped
     Freshly ground black pepper
½   teaspoon dried thyme
1   (15-ounce/430 g) can lentils, drained and rinsed, or 1½ cups (300 g) cooked lentils
¼   cup (60 ml) vegan mayo, store-bought or homemade (page 277)
2   tablespoons soy sauce
2   teaspoons fresh lemon juice
2   teaspoons smoked paprika
2   cups (200 g) breadcrumbs
½   cup (40 g) finely chopped walnuts
6   buns
     Lettuce, tomato slices, onions, and pickles, or whatever you love to put on burgers

Makes 6 burgers

1.   Preheat a large nonstick pan (preferably cast-iron) over medium-high heat. Sauté the onion in the olive oil for about 3 minutes with a pinch of salt. Add the mushrooms, pepper to taste, and thyme and sauté for 7 to 10 minutes more, until the mushrooms are soft and browned.

2.   In a food processor fit with a metal blade, puree the lentils with the mayo, soy sauce, lemon juice, and smoked paprika until relatively smooth. Add the mushroom mixture and half (only half!) of the breadcrumbs to the food processor and pulse to combine, but do not puree until smooth; leave a little bit of texture.

3.   Transfer the burger mixture to a large mixing bowl and add the remaining ½ cup (50 g) breadcrumbs and the walnuts, stirring to thoroughly combine. The mixture should hold its shape very well. Chill in the fridge for about 30 minutes to firm it up.

4.   Divide the burger mix into 6 equal pieces. An easy way to do this is divide it in half, then cut each half into 3 equal portions. You can do that right in the bowl if it's large enough. Form the 6 portions into patties.

5.   Lightly grease a large cast-iron pan with nonstick cooking spray. Cook the burgers on each side until lightly browned, about 10 minutes total. Assemble the burgers with the buns and toppings.

Chickpea Tuna Melt with Avocado and Dill

Yeah, a tuna melt is good, but have you had one with avocado and dill? Now that's a lunch! Or a dinner. Or a midnight snack. Vegan tuna salad has been around for a while, and it's an extremely important building block of the vegan culinary world. Many a person has been seen eating it out of Tupperware in front of the fridge at 1 A.M. But scoop it onto warm toasty bread, smother it in cashew cheese, and place some fresh dill on top and it becomes a whole new game. Very Lower East Side Jewish deli circa 1993. You can use store-bought vegan cheese instead of homemade, obviously.

Ingredients

Makes 6 open-face
sandwiches

1   (15-ounce/430 g) can chickpeas, drained and rinsed, or 1½ cups (240 g) cooked chickpeas
¼   cup (60 ml) vegan mayo, store-bought or homemade (page 277)
¼   teaspoon salt
    Freshly ground black pepper
¼   cup (35 g) finely chopped fresh dill
1   tablespoon dried onion flakes
1   medium carrot, peeled and very finely chopped
1   rib celery, finely chopped
6   slices thick crusty bread
½   recipe Meadow Cheese (page 106), at room temperature
2   avocados, peeled, pitted, and sliced
½   cup (15 g) loosely packed fresh dill sprigs
    Flaky sea salt, such as Maldon brand (optional)

1.   Preheat the oven to 425°F (220°C). Put the chickpeas in a mixing bowl and use an avocado masher or a strong fork to mash them well. They should retain some of their texture and not appear pureed. Leaving a few whole chickpeas is okay. Mix in the mayo, salt, and pepper to taste and mash a little bit more. Fold in the dill and onion flakes. Mix in the carrot and celery. Taste for salt and seasoning.

2.   Arrange the bread slices on a baking sheet. Bake them for 3 to 5 minutes, just to get them a little toasty. Remove the bread from the oven, handling the slices carefully because they will be hot. Let cool until you can comfortably handle them.

3.   Spread about ¼ cup (60 g) of the tuna salad onto each slice. Spoon on the cheese, dividing it equally among the slices. Return the baking sheet to the oven for 8 to 10 minutes, until the cheese is melty and hot.

4.   Transfer the tuna melts to plates and top with slices of avocado, fresh dill, and a sprinkling of flaky sea salt and extra black pepper, if desired.

Autumn Seitan Salad Sandwich

Thyme, cranberries, and celery work to create a sandwich that tastes a little like a Thanksgiving dinner—and, in fact, this sandwich is inspired by holiday pregaming. It's my favorite recipe to turn to as soon as the leaves start to change colors. I don't usually say this, but the fresh thyme is crucial here. Dried just doesn't have that same woodsy flavor. Vegan pretzel buns are widely available these days, and that's my absolute fave to use for these, but honestly any old bun will do. Or just enjoy the the seitan salad on top of a pile of arugula if you need more greens.

Ingredients

Makes 4 sandwiches

1   small yellow onion, chopped into medium dice
½   cup (50 g) thinly sliced celery
2   tablespoons olive oil
½   teaspoon salt, plus more for sautéing
1   (8-ounce/225 g) package seitan, chopped
1   tablespoon chopped fresh thyme
    Freshly ground black pepper
3   tablespoons vegan mayo, store-bought or homemade (page 277)
2   teaspoons Dijon mustard
¼   cup (35 g) fruit-sweetened dried cranberries
4   pretzel buns
    Big handful baby arugula

1.   Preheat a large cast-iron pan over medium heat. Sauté the onion and celery in the oil with a pinch of salt for about 3 minutes, just until slightly softened. Add the seitan, thyme, ½ teaspoon salt, and pepper to taste. Cook for about 10 minutes, flipping the seitan occasionally, until it is browned.

2.   In a mixing bowl, stir together the mayo and mustard. Transfer the cooked seitan mixture to the bowl and toss to coat. Fold in the cranberries. Let cool a bit.

3.   Split the pretzel buns in half and fill the sandwiches with the seitan salad and a little arugula.

Beer-Braised Tofu Tacos with Spinach

I love these tacos because you don't need a ton of toppings, or any, really! The beauty is that the filling cooks in its own sauce, with minimal ingredients but maximum flavor. Cilantro, cumin, and tomato are all heightened through the addition of beer. A little guac and you are all set.

Ingredients

Serves 4

2   tablespoons olive oil
1   (14-ounce/400 g) package
        extra-firm tofu, cubed
     Salt
1   medium onion, thinly sliced
3   cloves garlic, minced
2   cups (360 g) chopped tomato
¼   cup (10 g) finely chopped
        fresh cilantro
1   tablespoon agave
2   tablespoons nutritional
        yeast flakes
2   teaspoons ground cumin
1   teaspoon chipotle powder
1   cup (240 ml) brown ale
1   tablespoon fresh lemon juice
4   cups (80 g) loosely packed
        baby spinach
8   (8-inch/20 cm) tortillas
     Guacamole, for serving
        (page 279; optional)

1.   Preheat a large cast-iron pan over medium heat. Once the pan is good and hot, apply 1 tablespoon olive oil in a thin layer. Add the tofu and sprinkle with a pinch of salt. Cook for about 7 minutes, tossing often and spraying with additional oil as necessary, until the tofu is nicely browned. Transfer it to a plate; you'll add it back later. Keep the pan on the heat.

2.   Sauté the onion in remaining 1 tablespoon olive oil with a pinch of salt for 5 to 7 minutes, until lightly browned. Add the garlic and cook for about a minute. Add the tomato, cilantro, 1 teaspoon salt, agave, nutritional yeast, cumin, and chipotle powder and cook for another 5 minutes, until the tomatoes are broken down and juicy.

3.   Pour in the beer and turn up the heat to medium-high. Once boiling and bubbly, cook for about 2 minutes to reduce the liquid, then lower the heat to medium. Return the tofu to the pan and toss to coat and heat through for a minute or two.

4.   Turn the heat off. Stir in the lemon juice. Add the spinach in handfuls, tossing after each addition to wilt the greens. Serve the filling in warmed tortillas topped with guacamole, if desired.

I Can Cook Vegan

Golden Grilled Cheese with Tomato

There's a special place in our hearts we reserve for grilled cheese. Actually, I believe it's about 90 percent of the heart. The crisp, buttery bread giving way to doughiness giving way to meltiness. I absolutely must have a tomato in there for a juicy bite, too. I like to use white bread for my grilled cheese, but, you know, go ahead and be your wholesome self and swap in whole-grain sprouted and ruin everything. Also, serve with Cream of Tomato Soup (page 126) to make life complete. The Meadow Cheese is kind of a play on cheddar—it's beautifully hued like a sunset over a Nebraska meadow.

For the Meadow Cheese

- 1½ cups (180 g) whole unroasted cashews (if you don't own a high-speed blender, see page 24)
- ½ cup (120 g) chopped roasted red peppers
- 2 tablespoons nutritional yeast flakes
- 2 tablespoons mellow white miso
- 1 tablespoon fresh lemon juice
- 2 teaspoons onion powder
- 1 teaspoon ground turmeric
- 1 teaspoon salt
- ¼ cup (60 ml) unrefined coconut oil, melted

For the sandwich

- 8 large slices white bread
- 8 slices tomato
- 2 to 3 tablespoons unrefined coconut oil
  Salt

Makes 4 sandwiches

1. Make the meadow cheese: In a high-speed blender, combine the cashews, ½ cup (120 ml) water, the red peppers, nutritional yeast, miso, lemon juice, onion powder, turmeric, salt, and coconut oil. Blend until completely smooth. The mixture gets very thick, so you will likely need to use the plunger that came with your high-speed blender. Scrape down the sides with a rubber spatula to make sure you get everything.

2. Make the sandwiches: Preheat a large nonstick skillet (preferably cast-iron) over medium heat. Spread about ¼ cup (60 g) of the cheese on each slice of bread. Place a slice or two of tomato on four of the bread slices, then close the sandwiches.

3. Melt a few tablespoons of coconut oil in the hot skillet and sprinkle with salt. Working in batches if necessary, place the sandwiches in the skillet and cook until golden brown, 3 to 5 minutes. Flip each sandwich, placing small dollops of coconut oil underneath each one, and cook until golden brown on the second side. Serve immediately.

I Can Cook Vegan

Sloppy Shiitakes

Time to get sloppy! I bet vegans eat sloppy joes at ten times the rate of omnivores. Do people even make sloppy joes with meat anymore? There are so many vegan versions out there, some with lentils, some with seitan, some that are made with raw ingredients that I don't even want to think about. So I decided to do something a little special here. Shiitakes and adzuki beans provide toothsome, chewy texture that I think puts this sandwich a few rungs up from the other joes out there.

Ingredients

1   yellow onion, chopped
      into small dice
1   red bell pepper, chopped
      into small dice
2   tablespoons olive oil
4   cloves garlic, minced
6   ounces (170 g) shiitake
      mushrooms, cut into
      pea-size pieces
1   (15-ounce/430 g) can adzuki
      beans, drained and rinsed, or
      1½ cups (345 g) cooked
      adzuki beans
1   tablespoon smoked paprika
1   teaspoon ground cumin
1   teaspoon salt
1   cup (240 ml) tomato sauce
2   teaspoons ground mustard
3   tablespoons pure maple syrup
4   soft burger buns

Serves 4

1. Preheat a 4-quart (3.8 L) pot over medium heat. Sauté the onion and red pepper in the oil for 7 to 10 minutes, until soft. Add the garlic and shiitakes and sauté for about 2 minutes more, until the mushrooms are soft.

2. Mash the adzuki beans in a mixing bowl. They should be broken down by about half, not totally pureed, and have some individual beans still recognizable.

3. Add the paprika, cumin, and salt to the pot with the vegetables and toss to coat. Mix in the tomato sauce and heat through. Stir in the mustard and maple syrup and cook for 10 minutes more to allow the flavors to marry. Taste for salt and seasoning. Serve on the buns.

I Can Cook Vegan

Chickpea Egg Salad Sandwiches

Honestly, you could feed this to your grandma for dinner at 4:30 in the afternoon and she would just think it was a great egg salad sandwich. The usual suspects, kala namak and turmeric, make chickpeas incredibly eggy. And the texture is just right, too!

Ingredients

1   (15-ounce/430 g) can chickpeas, drained and rinsed, or 1½ cups (240 g) cooked chickpeas
¼   cup (60 ml) vegan mayo, store-bought or homemade (page 277), plus extra for spreading on toast
2   teaspoons kala namak (Indian black salt)
½   teaspoon ground turmeric
      Freshly ground black pepper
1   medium carrot, peeled and very finely chopped
1   rib celery, finely chopped
½   cup (65 g) finely chopped red onion
8   slices whole wheat toast
      Tomato slices
      Romaine lettuce leaves

Makes 4 sandwiches

1. Put the chickpeas in a mixing bowl and use an avocado masher or a strong fork to mash them well. They should retain some of their texture and not appear pureed. Leaving a few whole chickpeas is okay.

2. Mix in the mayo, kala namak, turmeric, and pepper to taste. Mash a little bit more. Fold in the carrot, celery, and red onion.

3. Assemble the chickpea salad and toast into sandwiches with lettuce and tomato.

I Can Cook Vegan

Tricolore Pizza

This pizza will not make anyone sad. It's got flavor on top of flavor! Pesto, red sauce, and a melty mozz sauce on top. Plus, cherry tomatoes that roast right into it (use multicolored ones if you can find them) and fresh basil leaves to complete your entire world. I know how annoying it is to have to flip through different pages to make one recipe, but listen: It's pizza, it's worth it. Pizza is totally manageable on a weeknight as long as you've got your crust ready. So go ahead and purchase pizza dough from your fave pizza dough store (you know, Trader Joe's or Whole Foods) and don't even worry about it. I'm telling you this because yeasted dough is a whole other thing that this book hasn't even touched on, but I still really, really want you to make pizza, and so this is a perfect entry point—starting at second base, if you will. On the off chance you are DYYYYIIINNG to make your dough from scratch, there are plenty of dependable recipes on the internet, some even written by me. Make the dough a day in advance so you can have this ready to rock for dinner the next day. I'm also going to go ahead and assume you don't have a pizza stone, a pizza pan, or anything that involves hobbyist pizza-making, so just bake the pizza on a flat baking sheet, no big whoop.

Ingredients

Flour for sprinkling
2   store-bought pizza doughs, at room temperature
2   cups (480 ml) marinara sauce, store-bought or homemade (page 278)
1   recipe Pesto (page 56)
1   recipe Melty Mozzy (page 274)
1   cup (145 g) halved cherry tomatoes
    Olive oil for drizzling
2   handfuls fresh basil leaves

Makes 2 pizzas

1.   Preheat the oven to 500°F (260°C). Lightly grease a large rimless baking sheet or pizza pan.

2.   Lightly flour a cold, clean surface for rolling the dough. Place the dough on the surface and shape into a disc, then use a floured rolling pin to roll it out about 14 inches (35.5 cm) wide. It's OK if it's not perfectly round! Transfer to the baking sheet.

3.   Spread 1 cup (240 ml) or so of the marinara on the pizza, leaving about 1 inch (2.5 cm) of crust around. Spoon about five dollops of pesto onto the pizza.

4.   Drizzle Melty Mozzy over everything. Place cherry tomatoes artfully across the pizza and drizzle a little olive oil on top.

5.   Place the pizza on the bottom of the oven (yes, right on the bottom, no rack required). Bake for about 10 minutes, or until the crust is golden. Remove from the oven. It will be very hot (obviously!), so be careful. Add the basil. When cool enough to handle, slide the pizza onto a cutting board and slice. Then make your next one the same way!

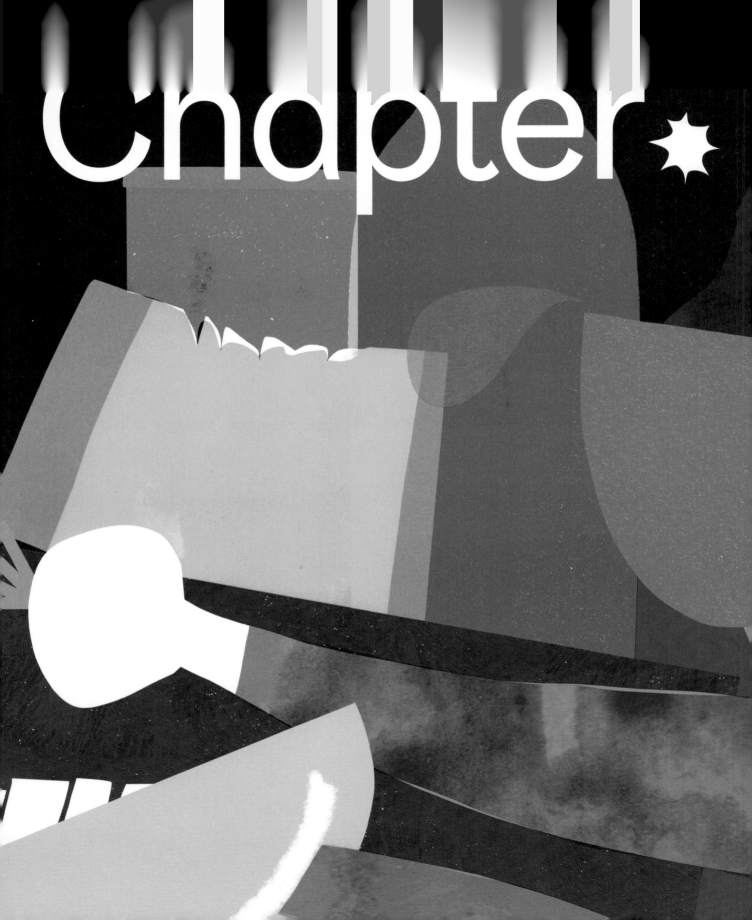

Chapter ✷

Soups & Stews

Mission: You'll work on your knife cuts and perfect your sauté skills. If you're the type of person who burns things, that will stop here and now as you learn to conduct and adjust your heat.* You'll also develop flavors, focusing on aromatics and seasoning. That seems like a lot, but you're ready for it!

* For instance, did you know you can shut the flame completely off?!

Soups and stews are probably the first thing you think of when you think of comfort food. Who doesn't crave spoonfuls from a big, steamy bowl of deliciousness on a rainy day? They fill your kitchen with the most wonderful aromas. The beauty for the beginner cook is that you'll use mostly pantry ingredients and simple equipment. And, of course, although not all of these recipes are one-pot, there is the benefit of the one-pot meal. Having everything simmering away on the stove top in a big soup pot is nice for the obvious reason—there's only one pot to clean! But the convenience of making a soup or stew goes beyond that—it's only one thing to think about, and that peace of mind is important. You don't have to worry about a sauce boiling over or a small oven fire. Just. This. One. Pot. Whether you want to make a creamy soup or a hearty curry, break out your favorite pot and let's get cooking!

I Can Cook Vegan

Soup tools

All of these recipes call for a 4-quart (3.8 L) pot. I use a stainless steel one with a nice big handle.

Always have a potholder or oven mitt at the ready! That handle gets hot and you're gonna wanna grab it to keep everything stable while you stir away. This seems obvious, but 30 years into cooking and I'm still always carelessly grabbing things. Don't be me!

My preferred tool for stirring is a slanted wooden spatula. It's plenty sturdy and can reach into the corners of the pan in case anything delicious is hidden there.

Soup tips

Ever burn the bottom of a pot and swear off soup altogether? You probably didn't deglaze! I request that you deglaze in this chapter more than any other! Deglazing is when you add a cold liquid (wine, broth, water, beer) to the hot aromatics in the pan to loosen them up. Then you can gently scrape the bottom of the pan to get all that yumminess. Happy pot, happy life.

Another way to make sure that the bottom of your pan doesn't burn is to stir often and keep the heat at a good, not-too-high level. That sounds obvious, but it's easy to forget if you're doing a million things or just browsing the internet for area rugs.

For the best soup and stew experience, let them sit for 10 minutes or so after cooking so the flavors can marry as they cool. If you can't wait, fine, but don't burn your mouth, either.

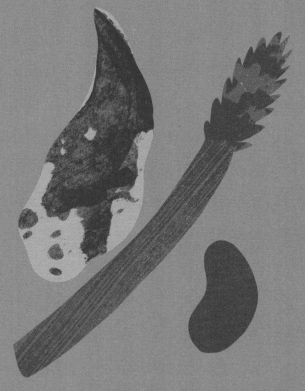

Mushroom-Lentil Noodle Soup

Noodle soups are the best because they're everything you love about an entree without any of the fuss. You've got your carbs, protein, and veggies all in one place! In this recipe, creminis and brown lentils team up to create a beefy soup that hits all the noodly notes. I love cavatappi because it holds its own with all of the hearty ingredients and won't fall apart if you have leftovers. If you can't find it, fusilli would be nice, too. Using dried lentils is crucial here to create a rich, complex broth, so don't sub cooked lentils, lazypants. There's a lot of finger-wagging on the best way to clean mushrooms. If you're on a tel-evised cooking competition, sure go ahead and wipe each precious one with a damp kitchen towel that has no cat hair on it. But if you're in the privacy of your own kitchen, go ahead and wash them in a bowl with cold water, swishing them around a bit to get the dirt off, then drain, trim, and slice. It's okay if they get waterlogged because, guess what, they're going in soup anyway.

Ingredients

Serves 6

- 1 medium yellow onion, thinly sliced
- 2 ribs celery, sliced ¼ inch (6 mm) thick
- 1 tablespoon olive oil
- 3 cloves garlic, minced
- 10 ounces (280 g) cremini mushrooms, thinly sliced (3 cups/185 g)
- ½ teaspoon salt
  Freshly ground black pepper
- 2 tablespoons chopped fresh thyme, plus extra for garnish
- 1½ cups (165 g) peeled carrots, sliced on a bias ¼ inch (6 mm) thick
- 8 cups (2 L) vegetable broth
- ½ cup (95 g) brown or green lentils
- 8 ounces (225 g) cavatappi or fusilli

1. Preheat a 4-quart (3.8 L) soup pot over medium heat. Sauté the onion and celery in the oil with a pinch of salt until soft, about 5 minutes. Add the garlic and cook until fragrant, 30 seconds or so.

2. Add the mushrooms, salt, pepper to taste, and the thyme and sauté until the mushrooms are soft and golden, about 5 minutes.

3. Add the carrots, vegetable broth, and lentils. Cover and bring to a boil. Once boiling, lower the heat to a simmer and cook until the lentils are tender, about 20 minutes, depending on your lentils.

4. Turn the heat up to a low boil, add the pasta, and cook for about 10 minutes, or until the pasta is done. Turn off the heat and let sit for 10 minutes. Taste for salt and pepper and serve.

I Can Cook Vegan

Garlicky White Bean and Asparagus Soup

One bite of asparagus and your surroundings transform into springtime. Birds start singing, bunnies start hopping around, you know the drill. It's a magical stalk and pureeing brings out the fresh flavor even more! This soup manages to be simple and also impressively elegant. Creamy, bright green, and just what you want to slurp when the trees are budding but there's still a little chill in the air. Asparagus spears range from pencil-thin to marker-fat in size. If you've got a choice, go somewhere in between for this recipe.

Ingredients

Serves 6

1   bunch asparagus (about 12 ounces/340 g), tough bottoms removed, tips trimmed off (about 2 inches/5 cm), stems thinly sliced
1   tablespoon olive oil, plus extra for serving
1   medium yellow onion, cut into medium dice
6   cloves garlic, chopped
½   teaspoon dried tarragon
½   teaspoon salt
    Freshly ground pepper
¼   cup (13 g) chopped fresh chives, plus extra for garnish
4   cups (960 ml) vegetable broth
1   (15-ounce/430 g) can navy beans, drained and rinsed, or 1½ cups (275 g) cooked navy beans
1   tablespoon fresh lemon juice

1. Preheat a 4-quart (3.8 L) soup pot over medium heat. Sauté the asparagus tips in the oil with a pinch of salt for about 3 minutes. Remove about 10 of them for garnish and set aside.

2. Turn the heat up a bit, add the asparagus stems, onion, garlic, tarragon, salt, and pepper to taste and sauté for about 5 minutes, until the onion is soft and the garlic is golden. Add the chives, broth, beans, and lemon juice and bring to a boil for 3 minutes.

3. Transfer to a blender and puree until completely smooth. The soup will be very hot, so turn off the blender and remove the lid every 10 seconds or so to let steam escape. Serve in bowls and garnish with the asparagus tips, extra chives, and a swoosh of olive oil.

I Can Cook Vegan

Cream of Mushroom Soup

This is total luxury for mushroom lovers. The kind of soup that tastes like you've just returned from cooking classes abroad. But the truth is: garlic, white wine, and mushrooms are pure umami. If you'd like to get even fancier, substitute half (or all) of the creminis with oyster mushrooms or anything tickling your fancy at the farmers' market. All of the attitude of a culinary degree with none of the debt!

Ingredients

Serves 6

- 1 medium yellow onion, chopped into medium dice
- 3 cloves garlic, chopped
- 2 tablespoons refined coconut oil
- 1 (10-ounce/280 g) package cremini mushrooms, sliced
- 2 tablespoons chopped fresh thyme
  Freshly ground black pepper
- ½ cup (60 ml) dry white wine
- 4 cups (960 ml) vegetable broth
- ½ cup (60 g) whole unroasted cashews (if you don't own a high-speed blender, see page 24)
- 3 cups (60 g) loosely packed baby arugula
  Truffle oil, for serving (optional)

1. Preheat a 4-quart (3.8 L) pot over medium heat. Sauté the onion and garlic in the coconut oil with a pinch of salt, just until softened, about 5 minutes. Add mushrooms and sauté until softened, another 5 minutes. Remove ½ cup (80 g) of the mushroom slices to use for garnish, if you like.

2. Stir in the thyme and pepper to taste. Add the white wine and use a spatula to deglaze the pan. Turn up the heat a bit and cook for 3 minutes to reduce the alcohol. Mix in the broth and turn off the heat.

3. Place the cashews in a high-speed blender. Add everything from the mushroom pot. Blend until completely smooth. The soup will be very hot, so turn off the blender and remove the lid every 10 seconds or so to let steam escape and to scrape down the sides with a rubber spatula.

4. Return the soup to the pot over low heat to warm through and thicken, 3 to 5 minutes. Taste for salt. Transfer to bowls and garnish each serving with the reserved mushrooms. Top with arugula and drizzle with truffle oil, if you've got it. Finish with black pepper.

Cream of Tomato Soup with Noochy Croutons

All right, I've already mentioned rainy days and nostalgia, and I guess all soups have that going for them. However! How can I not repeat myself when it comes to cream of tomato soup? It personifies the comfort, ease, and therapeutic qualities of soup. This version gets a little kick from red pepper flakes, and the zestiest tomato flavor from using whole canned tomatoes. Serve with Golden Grilled Cheese with Tomato (page 106), if you like. The cheesy Noochy Croutons (page 281) will hit the spot, too. I love canned fire-roasted tomatoes, which are easy enough to find these days, but plain old canned tomatoes will serve you just fine.

Ingredients

Serves 6

1   yellow onion, chopped into medium dice
5   cloves garlic, minced
1   teaspoon dried thyme
1   teaspoon dried rosemary
½   teaspoon red pepper flakes (optional)
2   tablespoons olive oil, plus more for serving
4   cups (960 ml) vegetable broth
1   (25-ounce/720 g) can whole fire-roasted tomatoes
2   tablespoons tomato paste
½   teaspoon salt
    Freshly ground black pepper
½   cup (60 g) whole unroasted cashews (if you don't own a high-speed blender, see page 24)
1   recipe Noochy Croutons (optional; page 281)
    Sliced chives, for serving

1. Preheat a 4-quart (3.8 L) pot over medium heat. Sauté the onion, garlic, thyme, rosemary, and red pepper flakes (if desired) in the olive oil with a pinch of salt, just until softened, about 3 minutes. Add the vegetable broth, can of tomatoes, tomato paste, salt, and pepper to taste and mash with a potato masher or spatula, just to get the tomatoes slightly broken up. Turn the heat up and cook until hot and bubbly, about 10 minutes.

2. Place the cashews in a high-speed blender. Add everything from the tomato pot. Blend until completely smooth. The soup will be very hot, so turn off the blender and remove the lid every 10 seconds or so to let steam escape and to scrape down the sides with a rubber spatula.

3. Return the soup to the pot over low heat and heat through. Serve hot with a little olive oil drizzled over the top. Add croutons, if desired, and sprinkle with sliced chives.

I Can Cook Vegan

Sweet Potato Soup with Ginger and Lime

Enjoy this at the Thanksgiving table or from a thermos at your desk! Either way, you will be in autumny bliss. Sweet potatoes whip up into the silkiest, creamiest soup. There's such a great balance here between the kick of the ginger, the sweetness of the potatoes, and the tart lime. It's autumn perfection in its simplest, soupiest form.

Ingredients

Serves 6

1   cup (140 g) roughly chopped shallots
1   tablespoon refined coconut oil
2   tablespoons chopped fresh ginger
¼   teaspoon red pepper flakes
3   pounds (1.4 kg) garnet yams, peeled and cut into 1-inch (2.5 cm) chunks
4   cups (960 ml) vegetable broth
½   teaspoon salt
1   tablespoon pure maple syrup
¼   cup (60 ml) fresh lime juice
     Lime wedges, for serving

1.   Preheat a 4-quart (3.8 L) pot over medium heat. Sauté the shallots in the coconut oil with a pinch of salt, just until softened, about 3 minutes. Add the ginger and red pepper flakes and sauté another minute or so.

2.   Add the yams, veggie broth, and salt. Cover and bring to a boil. Once boiling, lower the heat a bit to a slow simmer and cook until the potatoes are tender—usually about 5 minutes.

3.   Use an immersion blender to puree the soup until smooth, or transfer the soup in batches to a blender or food processor to puree. Be sure to take the lid off between pulses so that the steam doesn't build up in the blender. Then transfer the soup back to the pot.

4.   Stir in the maple syrup and lime juice and taste for salt. Thin with a little water, if necessary. Serve with more lime wedges.

I Can Cook Vegan

Tortilla Soup with Black Beans and Artichokes

This soup is pure fun! It's got so many flavors and textures. I chose artichokes to kinda mimic the way chicken pulls apart in tortilla soup but cruelty-free style. The usual tortilla soup suspects are also present: jalapeño, cilantro, tomato, corn, and black beans. It's a perfectly crowd-pleasing weeknight meal that's hard not to turn to when you don't want tacos for the sixth night in a row. Trimming, prepping, and steaming artichokes yourself is an infinitely better way to eat an artichoke. However, this book isn't about taking 3 hours to make one recipe. So when I'm cooking with pre-prepped artichokes, I choose frozen ones over canned or jarred. The flavor is better because they're not packed with oils or brine. Another bonus? Frozen is cheaper. I always thaw them before using the recipe, which is easy; just put them in the fridge the night before.

Ingredients

Serves 6

1   medium red onion, thinly sliced
2   jalapeños, seeded and minced, plus extra for garnish
2   tablespoons olive oil
4   cloves garlic, minced
½   cup (20 g) chopped fresh cilantro, plus extra for garnish
1   tablespoon ground cumin
1   teaspoon salt
1   (24-ounce/680 g) can diced tomatoes
3   cups (720 ml) vegetable broth
1   (25-ounce/710 g) can black beans, drained and rinsed
1   cup (135 g) frozen corn
1   (10-ounce/280 g) package frozen artichoke hearts, thawed (see headnote)
4   cups (320 g) crushed corn tortillas chips
     Lime wedges, for squeezing
     Hot sauce, for serving

1. Preheat a 4-quart (3.8 L) pot over medium heat. Sauté the onion and jalapeños in the olive oil with a pinch of salt, until lightly browned, about 5 minutes. Add the garlic and cilantro and sauté for a minute or so, until the cilantro is very wilted. Mix in the cumin and cook until toasty, about 30 seconds.

2. Add the salt, tomatoes, and broth. Cover and increase the heat to high to bring to a boil.

3. Once boiling, add the beans, corn, and artichoke hearts. Turn the heat down to low and simmer, covered, for 5 minutes.

4. Taste for salt and seasoning. Serve with crushed-up chips on top and a squeeze of lime, and garnish with extra jalapeños and cilantro. And don't forget the hot sauce!

Yellow Split Pea Soup with Grilled Eggplant

Split pea soup begs for something smoky and grilled eggplant is there for it! Don't be fooled by the short ingredient list for the base recipe; yellow split peas have a unique flavor that is a little more savory than green, to my taste buds anyway. I also love the golden hue! If you want to go even simpler and forgo the eggplant, a little sprinkle of smoked paprika will do the trick. I use Japanese eggplants because they're thinner than European varieties, and even more purple. The result is a smaller, brighter garnish that's very easy to prep and rests easily on a bowl of soup without sinking. Did I mention that they're more purple?

For the soup

1	medium onion, cut into small dice
1	tablespoon olive oil
4	cloves garlic, minced
	Freshly ground black pepper
1	teaspoon salt
½	teaspoon dried thyme
2	cups (240 g) baby carrots, sliced on a bias ¼ inch (6 mm) thick
1¼	cups (245 g) yellow split peas
6	cups (1.4 L) vegetable broth
	Thinly sliced chives, for garnish

For the eggplant

2	small Japanese eggplants, sliced ¼ inch (6 mm) thick
2	tablespoons olive oil
¼	teaspoon salt
	Freshly ground black pepper

Serves 6

1. Make the soup: Preheat a 4-quart (3.8 L) soup pot over medium-high heat. Sauté the onion in the oil until translucent, about 5 minutes. Add the garlic, pepper to taste, salt, and thyme and sauté another minute.

2. Add the carrots, split peas, and broth. Cover the pot and bring to a boil, keeping a close eye. Once it's boiling, lower the heat to a simmer and cook for about 40 minutes, until the lentils are tender.

3. In the meantime, make the eggplant: Preheat a cast-iron grill or grill pan over medium heat. In a large mixing bowl, toss the eggplant with the olive oil, salt, and pepper.

4. Spray the grill or grill pan generously with nonstick cooking spray. Grill the eggplant slices on each side until grill marks appear, about 3 minutes.

5. Taste the soup for salt and seasoning. Serve in bowls topped with eggplant slices and chives.

Smoky Tomato Lentil Soup with Spinach and Olives

Olives are an underutilized soup ingredient and I demand they have their day in the broth! They add bright bursts of briny flavor to this sultry tomato lentil soup and really enhance the whole thing with a Mediterranean flair. Spinach wilted in at the end means you've got all your nutrition in one pot. This will be a really nice addition to your lentil soup repertoire. Since olives are salty, wait until after you've added them to the soup to decide if you need more salt. You can use hot smoked paprika instead of sweet, but do remember that it's hot! So your soup is gonna be spicy. Start with a tablespoon and go from there.

Ingredients

Serves 6

- 1 yellow onion, thinly sliced
- 1 tablespoon olive oil
  Salt
- 3 cloves garlic, minced
- 1 teaspoon dried thyme
- 2 tablespoons sweet smoked paprika (see headnote)
- 1 cup (190 g) brown or green lentils
- 5 cups (1.2 L) vegetable broth
  Freshly ground black pepper
- 1 (24-ounce/680 g) can stewed tomatoes (fire-roasted, if you can find them)
- 4 cups (80 g) loosely packed baby spinach or chopped spinach
- ¾ cup (115 g) pitted, roughly chopped Kalamata olives

1. Preheat a 4-quart (3.8 L) soup pot over medium-high heat. Sauté the onion in the oil with a pinch of salt until translucent, about 5 minutes. Add the garlic and thyme and sauté for 30 seconds or so, until fragrant.

2. Add the paprika, lentils, broth, ½ teaspoon salt, and pepper to taste. Cover and bring to a boil. Once boiling, turn the heat to medium and cook for 25 minutes, stirring occasionally, until the lentils are almost tender.

3. Add the tomatoes. Bring to a boil again, then lower the heat to a simmer for another 20 minutes or so, or until the lentils are very tender. Add the spinach and olives and stir frequently until the spinach is wilted and velvety. Add water to thin, if necessary. Taste for salt and seasoning.

I Can Cook Vegan

Baingan Bharta

The smokiest, most lush curry ever! Roasting an eggplant to death gives it lots of charred flavor that shines through a bouquet of fragrant spice. It's not a one-pot meal, but roasting the eggplant is a simple method that yields impressive results. If you'd like to make this dish even more filling, try adding kidney beans, chickpeas, or black-eyed peas.

Ingredients

Serves 6

- 2 pounds (910 g) eggplant (about 3 medium-size)
- 3 tablespoons refined coconut oil
- 1 medium onion, chopped into medium dice
- 3 cloves garlic, peeled and finely chopped
- 2 tablespoons minced fresh ginger
- 2 jalapeños, finely diced, plus extra for garnish
- ½ cup (20 g) finely chopped fresh cilantro, plus extra for garnish
- 1 tablespoon mild curry powder
- 2 teaspoons smoked paprika
- 1 teaspoon garam masala
- 1 teaspoon salt
- 1 (25-ounce/710 g) can crushed tomatoes
- 1 tablespoon agave
- 3 tablespoons fresh lime juice
  Unsweetened plain coconut yogurt, for serving (optional)

1. Preheat the oven to 450°F (230°C). Line a baking sheet with parchment paper. Poke the eggplants all over with a fork about 10 times each. Rub with 2 tablespoons of the coconut oil and place on the prepared baking sheet. Bake until collapsed, about 40 minutes.

2. Let the eggplants cool just until you can handle them without burning yourself. Remove the skin and discard. Chop up the eggplant into roughly ¾-inch (2 cm) pieces. Place in a bowl so you don't lose any of the juice.

3. Preheat a 4-quart (3.8 L) soup pot over medium-high heat. Sauté the onion in the remaining tablespoon of coconut oil with a pinch of salt until translucent, about 5 minutes. Add the garlic, ginger, and jalapeños and sauté for another 3 minutes.

4. Add the cilantro and sauté until wilted. Add the curry powder, paprika, garam masala, and salt and toss them to coat the onions.

5. Add the tomatoes and eggplant and mix well, scraping the bottom of the pan to deglaze. Cover the pan and bring the heat up a bit. Cook for another 15 minutes or so.

6. Stir in the agave and lime juice. Serve topped with coconut yogurt, if desired, and additional cilantro and/or jalapeño (if you like it spicy!).

I Can Cook Vegan

Chickpea Potato Curry with Peas

There are times when you want to break out the mortar and pestle and make your own curry powder. And then there are Tuesdays. If you don't have a basic, go-to curry in your life, maybe you need one. You should be able to open your cupboard, pull out a few cans of this, a few jars of that, and be halfway done with the recipe. This is the kind of stew that will have you waking up in the middle of the night to eat it cold, right out of the fridge. This will only be as delicious as your favorite curry powder, so make sure you choose a top-quality blend whose first ingredient is not "yellow #5." Serve with basmati rice and a store-bought chutney, if you like.

Ingredients

Serves 6

1½ cups (210 g) trimmed and peeled medium-dice shallots
1 tablespoon coconut oil
4 cloves garlic, minced
1 tablespoon minced fresh ginger
¼ cup (10 g) chopped fresh cilantro, plus extra for garnish
2 tablespoons mild curry powder
2 teaspoons ground cumin
¼ teaspoon red pepper flakes
3 cups (720 ml) vegetable broth
1 tablespoon agave
1 teaspoon salt
1 large carrot, peeled and sliced on a bias ¼ inch (6 mm) thick
12 ounces Yukon Gold potatoes, cut into ¾-inch (2 cm) cubes
1 (15-ounce/425 g) can chickpeas, drained and rinsed, or 1½ cups (240 g) cooked chickpeas
1 (15-ounce/440 ml) can full-fat coconut milk
1 cup (135 g) frozen peas

1. Preheat a 4-quart (3.8 L) pot over medium heat. Sauté the shallots in the coconut oil for about 5 minutes, until lightly browned.

2. Add the garlic and ginger and sauté until fragrant, about 30 seconds. Add the cilantro, curry powder, cumin, red pepper flakes, broth, agave, and salt and give it a stir.

3. Add the carrot and potatoes, cover the pot, and bring to a boil. Once boiling, immediately lower the heat to a simmer and leave the lid ajar so that steam can escape. Let the potatoes cook just until tender, about 5 minutes more.

4. Once the potatoes are tender, add the chickpeas, coconut milk, and frozen peas and heat through. Serve garnished with cilantro.

I Can Cook Vegan

Creamy Chickpea Bow Tie Soup

This has chicken pot pie vibes, what with the creaminess, green peas, carrots, and thyme. It's got just the right amount of cashew cream to make it decadent, but it's still brothy and soupy enough to make for a light but filling lunch (or dinner, or second breakfast). Bow ties, or farfalle, always remind me of grandmothers, so tell the jealous people in your office that they can't have the recipe because it was passed down to your grandma from her grandma. Serve with crusty bread because carbs plus carbs equal hearts. You can use peeled baby carrots instead of peeling your own carrots here (and for most recipes in the book, while we're at it).

Ingredients

Serves 6

1	medium yellow onion, thinly sliced
1	tablespoon olive oil
	Salt
3	cloves garlic, minced
2	tablespoons chopped fresh thyme, plus extra for garnish
6	cups (1.4 L) vegetable broth
1	cup (140 g) peeled carrots, chopped into ¾-inch (2 cm) chunks
1	cup (55 g) farfalle
	Freshly ground black pepper
½	cup (60 g) whole unroasted cashews (if you don't own a high-speed blender, see page 24)
1	(24-ounce/680 g) can chickpeas, drained and rinsed
1	cup (135 g) frozen peas

1. Preheat a 4-quart (3.8 L) soup pot over medium heat. Sauté onion in the oil with a pinch of salt until soft, about 5 minutes. Add garlic and thyme and cook until fragrant, 30 seconds or so.

2. Add broth and carrots and bring to a boil.

3. Once boiling, add pasta, 1 teaspoon salt, and pepper to taste. Cook until pasta is done, about 8 minutes.

4. In the meantime, place cashews in a high-speed blender with 1 cup (240 ml) water. Blend until completely smooth, occasionally scraping down the sides with a rubber spatula to make sure you get everything.

5. When pasta is cooked, add chickpeas, cashew cream mixture, and peas. Lower heat and simmer for 5 minutes. Turn off heat and let sit for 10 minutes. Taste for salt and pepper and serve. Garnish with extra thyme.

Pearl's Bean and Barley Chili

Pearled barley gives this chili the heartiest texture. It also absorbs all the aromatic yumminess and makes for a mean bowl of chili. A little beer deglazes the pot and gives plenty of complexity in the easiest way. Chili is one of those recipes that you will probably make a few times a month, at least in the colder months, and I hope that you will tinker a bit, adding seasoning to your liking, finding the perfect chili powder, and customizing this recipe so much that you can name the chili after yourself. I love to top my chili with basically everything. Some ideas are crushed tortilla chips, avocado, chopped tomato, and fresh cilantro.

Ingredients

Serves 8 to 10

1	medium yellow onion, chopped into medium dice
2	green bell peppers, chopped into medium dice
3	bay leaves
2	tablespoons olive oil
6	cloves garlic, minced
3	tablespoons mild chili powder
2	teaspoons dried Mexican oregano
1	tablespoon ground cumin
1½	teaspoons salt
½	teaspoon red pepper flakes
1	cup light-colored Mexican beer
¾	cup (150 g) pearled barley
3	cups (720 ml) vegetable broth
1	(28-ounce/800 g) can crushed tomatoes
1	(25-ounce/710 g) can kidney beans, drained and rinsed, or 2½ cups (400 g) cooked kidney beans
2	tablespoons fresh lime juice
1	tablespoon agave

1. Preheat a 4-quart (3.8 L) pot over medium-high heat. Sauté the onion, green pepper, and bay leaves in the oil with a pinch of salt for about 10 minutes, until the onion is lightly browned.

2. Add the garlic and sauté until fragrant, about 30 seconds. Add the chili powder, oregano, cumin, salt, and red pepper flakes and cook to toast the spices for about a minute.

3. Pour in the beer and scrape the bottom of the pan to deglaze. Let cook for about 2 minutes. Add the barley and vegetable broth and give it a good stir. Cover the pot, leaving the lid slightly ajar to let steam escape, and turn the heat up to bring it to a gentle boil. Boil until the barley is almost tender, stirring once in a while, about 15 minutes.

4. Add the crushed tomatoes and kidney beans. Cover the pot again and turn down the heat to a simmer. Let cook for about 20 minutes more, stirring occasionally. The barley should be very tender and the chili should be thick. Add a little water if necessary.

5. Add the lime juice and agave, then taste for salt and seasoning. Remove the bay leaves if you can find them. Serve with your choice of accoutrements.

I Can Cook Vegan

Sweet Potato Quinoa Stew with Kidney Beans

A brothy, satisfying soup that covers all the bases: beans, greens, and grains! Delicate flavors of ginger and rosemary let the main ingredients shine. Sweet potatoes cook way faster than regular potatoes, so this is a good lesson to learn. Keep your eye on the prize (the pot) and lower the heat as needed so the sweet potatoes don't boil too much and break apart.

Ingredients

Serves 6

1	cup (115 g) thinly sliced shallots
2	tablespoons olive oil
4	cloves garlic, minced
1	tablespoon grated fresh ginger
½	teaspoon dried rosemary
6	cups (1.4 L) vegetable broth
1½	pounds (680 g) sweet potatoes, peeled and cut into ¾-inch (2 cm) chunks
½	cup (85 g) quinoa
⅛	teaspoon cayenne
¾	teaspoon salt
1	(15-ounce/430 g) can kidney beans, drained and rinsed, or 1½ cups (265 g) cooked kidney beans
1	bunch (6 to 8 average-size stalks) lacinato kale, stripped from stems, torn into pieces

1. Preheat a 4-quart (3.8 L) pot over medium-high heat. Sauté the shallots in the oil with a pinch of salt for about 3 minutes, until translucent. Add the garlic, ginger, and rosemary and sauté until fragrant, about 30 seconds.

2. Add the broth and scrape the bottom of the pan to deglaze. Add the sweet potatoes, quinoa, cayenne, and salt. Turn the heat up a bit and cover the pot, leaving the lid slightly ajar for steam to escape, and bring to a low boil.

3. Once boiling, keep a close eye, lowering the heat if it gets too crazy, and cook until the sweet potatoes are fork tender and the quinoa is fluffy, 15 to 20 minutes.

4. Add the kidney beans and heat through, about 2 minutes. Add the kale, turn off the heat, and let the kale wilt in the hot stew. Serve!

Chapter

5

Bowls & Sautés

When Instagram thinks of vegan food, this is what they think about. A bowl that poureth over with greens, seeds, a grilled unidentifiable rectangle (G.U.R. for short), and a sauce, just out of frame, drizzling over everything. And there ain't nothin' wrong with that! Some of these recipes are quick stove-top throw-it-all-together deals, and some are multirecipe, mix-and-match bowls.

Mission: Multitasking. Whip up quick sauces to pull together other very simply prepared ingredients. This section will also teach you a lot about simple techniques: how to make perfectly cooked fluffy quinoa and roasted potatoes that are creamy on the inside. You'll have a few things going at once, and you'll keep track of all of them, effortlessly.

Sautéed Lentils with Dandelion Greens and Radicchio

If there aren't delicious aromatics wafting through the air, have you even cooked? I use this method on whatever I picked up at the anarchist co-op (okay, fine, Whole Foods) and whatever beans I have burning a hole in my cupboard. Try it with spinach, arugula, or chard, or try it with dandelion greens like the recipe says. It takes only 15 minutes or so and it tastes like it took 20. Shallots, onion, olive oil . . . now that's dinner!

Ingredients

Serves 4

- ½   cup (50 g) walnuts
- 1   cup (115 g) thinly sliced shallots
- 2   tablespoons olive oil
- 2   cloves garlic, minced
- ½   teaspoon dried tarragon
     Freshly ground black pepper
- 2   tablespoons nutritional yeast flakes
- ¼   cup (60 ml) dry white wine
- ½   cup (120 ml) vegetable broth
- 1   large bunch dandelion greens
- 1½ cups (300 g) cooked brown or green lentils
- 2   cups (80 g) thinly sliced radicchio

1.   Preheat the oven to 350°F (175°C). Spread the walnuts out on a small baking sheet and toast them for about 10 minutes. Let cool and roughly chop.

2.   In the meantime, preheat a large pan over medium heat. Sauté the shallots in the olive oil with a pinch of salt until lightly browned, about 5 minutes. Add the garlic, tarragon, and pepper to taste and sauté for another minute.

3.   Add the nutritional yeast and toast it, stirring with a wooden spatula, about 1 minute. Pour in the white wine and scrape the bottom of the pan to deglaze. Let cook for about 3 minutes more.

4.   Pour in the vegetable broth and bring to a boil. Add the greens and cook down for about 5 minutes. Add the lentils and toss to heat through. At the last moment, toss in the radicchio to wilt, then serve.

I Can Cook Vegan

Pesto Wild Rice with Fava Beans and Kale

Like most people, I first stir-fried grains with classic Chinese fried rice. Then I realized I could expand to other types of rice and, heck, even other grains! Flavors can be anything from Indian to Italian to . . . whatever you want. But let's just leave it on Italian for now. Fava beans often come frozen because they taste best that way. Just thaw them first. But don't worry if you forget—this recipe will just take a little longer to cook.

Ingredients

Serves 4

2	cloves garlic, minced
1	tablespoon olive oil
1	pound (455 g) purple kale, rough stems removed, torn into large pieces
4	cups (720 g) cooked and cooled wild rice
1	cup Pesto (page 56)
½	cup (120 ml) vegetable broth, plus more, as needed
1	tablespoon fresh lemon juice
½	teaspoon salt
	Freshly ground black pepper
2	cups (300 g) cooked fava beans
½	cup (60 g) chopped walnuts
	Fresh basil leaves, for garnish

1. Preheat a large heavy-bottomed pan (preferably cast-iron) over medium heat. Cook the garlic in the olive oil for about a minute. Add the kale and toss to wilt it, about 2 minutes.

2. Add the rice and toss to heat through, about 2 more minutes. Mix in the pesto, vegetable broth, lemon juice, salt, and pepper to taste. Let heat through for a minute.

3. Add the fava beans and toss to coat. Cook for about 5 minutes, until the kale is nicely cooked down and velvety but not mushy. Taste for salt and seasoning. Serve garnished with walnuts and basil.

Sausage and Peppers with Swiss Chard

I love sausage and peppers, and adding greens to them makes this pairing more like dinner and less like you're being incredibly naughty at the street fair. Plus, it's just so dang pretty! The earthiness of Swiss chard, the sweetness of the peppers and onion, the fennel-iness of the sausage . . . this is perfect Sunday night fare that you'll want in the center of the table. Some bread, some marinara—I'm not going to make stereotypical *Sopranos* jokes here because Italian food is so much more than that (but, oops, I just did).

Ingredients

Serves 4

4   Italian sausages, store-bought or homemade (page 275), sliced on a bias ½ inch (12 mm) thick
3   tablespoons olive oil
1   red bell pepper, cut into ¼-inch-thick (6 mm) slices
1   large yellow onion, cut into ¼-inch-thick (6 mm) slices
3   cloves garlic, minced
½   teaspoon salt
    Freshly ground black pepper
¼   teaspoon dried oregano
¼   teaspoon red pepper flakes
1   pound (455 g) Swiss chard, leaves torn into big pieces, stems thinly sliced
½   cup (120 ml) vegetable broth
1   tablespoon red wine vinegar

1.   Preheat a large heavy-bottomed pan (preferably cast-iron) over medium heat. Cook the sausage in 2 tablespoons of the olive oil, tossing to brown it on all sides, about 5 minutes. Transfer to a plate.

2.   Add the remaining 1 tablespoon oil to the pan and cook the red pepper and onion in a pinch of salt until lightly browned, 5 to 7 minutes. Add the garlic, salt, black pepper to taste, oregano, and red pepper flakes and cook for about 30 seconds. Add the Swiss chard and cook until wilted, about 3 minutes.

3.   Return the sausages to the pan with the vegetable broth and vinegar. Turn up the heat and heat through. Serve!

Beefy Tempeh and Broccoli

If you love beef and broccoli from your favorite Chinese takeout, then this savory gravy, deeply flavored with ginger and sesame, is the recipe for you! A little tangy, a little spicy, and definitely smothering every inch of the tempeh and broccoli.

Ingredients

Serves 4

½ cup (120 ml) cold vegetable broth
2 teaspoons cornstarch
¼ cup (60 ml) tamari
3 tablespoons hoisin sauce
2 tablespoons rice wine vinegar
1 tablespoon Sriracha sauce
1 pound (455 g) tempeh, sliced on a diagonal
3 tablespoons toasted sesame oil
1 cup (115 g) thinly sliced shallots
6 cups (540 g) broccoli florets
2 tablespoons minced fresh ginger
2 cloves garlic, minced

For serving

Brown rice
Toasted sesame seeds
Thinly sliced scallions (white and light green parts only)
Thinly sliced dried hot chile pepper (optional)

1. In a mug using a fork, mix the broth and cornstarch until well dissolved. Add the tamari, hoisin, rice wine vinegar, and Sriracha. Set the sauce aside.

2. Preheat a large skillet over medium-high heat. Cook the tempeh in 1 tablespoon of the sesame oil until seared on both sides, 7 to 10 minutes. Transfer the tempeh to a plate and set aside.

3. Add 1 tablespoon of the sesame oil to the skillet and cook the broccoli, stirring often, until softened, about 5 minutes.

4. Push the broccoli to the side and add the ginger and garlic to a clear spot. Drizzle the remaining tablespoon of sesame oil on the ginger and garlic and toss for about 30 seconds, just until fragrant, and then toss the aromatics together with the broccoli.

5. Return the tempeh to the pan. Pour in the reserved sauce, mix everything together, and increase the heat to bring it to a boil. Let the sauce thicken and reduce for about 3 minutes, then lower the heat and cook for another 2 minutes. Serve over rice, garnished with sesame seeds, scallions, and sliced dried pepper, if desired.

Tempeh and Brussels Sprouts with Sun-Dried Tomatoes

Nothing pleases me more than a quick one-pot sauté that also happens to have layers of flavor. Well, some things please me more, but after internet cats and world peace comes a weeknight meal like this. Lots of Mediterranean flavors here: sweet onions, loads of garlic, white wine, pungent sun-dried tomatoes, and briny capers. I love using tempeh in unexpected ways because its heartiness stands up to the dramatic ingredients. Here it's a perfect match for roasted and seared brussels sprouts, but you can use this method with so many other ingredients. I like to serve this with a bold whole grain, like farro or wheat berries, but it's also wonderful with mashed potatoes or rice. Or just on its glorious own!

Ingredients

Serves 4

1   (8-ounce/225 g) block tempeh, cut into medium dice
3   tablespoons olive oil
8   ounces (225 g) brussels sprouts, quartered
¼   cup (35 g) thinly sliced garlic
1   yellow onion, thinly sliced into half-moons
2   tablespoons fresh thyme
¼   cup (30 g) capers, drained
¼   cup (30 g) sun-dried tomatoes in oil, cut into ¼-inch-thick (6 mm) slices
½   cup (120 ml) dry white wine
1   cup (240 ml) vegetable broth
    Freshly ground black pepper

For serving

A hearty grain, like brown rice or barley
Chopped fresh flat-leaf parsley

1.   Preheat a large skillet over medium-high heat. Cook the tempeh in 1 tablespoon of the olive oil with a sprinkle of salt until seared on a few sides, 7 to 10 minutes. Transfer the tempeh to a plate and set aside.

2.   Add 1 tablespoon of the oil to the pan, place the brussels sprouts facedown in the oil, and sear them, about 5 minutes. Push to the side of the pan.

3.   Add the garlic to the pan, drizzle in the remaining tablespoon oil, and cook the garlic for about a minute, until lightly browned. Add the onion and thyme with a sprinkle of salt and toss to coat. Cook the onion for 5 to 7 minutes, until lightly browned. Circulate the brussels sprouts in the pan while you're at it.

4.   Add the capers and sun-dried tomatoes to the pan and toss to coat. Pour in the white wine and the broth and combine the sprouts with everything else. Add a healthy amount of black pepper. Increase the heat to high, bring to a boil, and let the wine reduce, about 3 minutes.

5.   Lower the heat and transfer the tempeh back to the pan, tossing to combine. Heat through for about a minute, then serve over grains and sprinkle with fresh parsley, if desired.

Polenta Puttanesca

Puttanesca is the ultimate pantry sauce. Usually reserved for pasta, in this bowl we're tossing it with seared tofu, capers, olives, and tomato with lots of garlic, oregano, basil, and a little spice. The soft polenta soaks up all the flavor! Add arugula for a little green and you've got a beautiful bowl of rustic Italian charm.

For the tofu puttanesca

- 2 tablespoons olive oil
- 1 (14-ounce/400 g) block extra-firm tofu, cut into cubes
- ½ teaspoon salt
- 4 cloves garlic, minced
- 1 (25-ounce/710 g) can crushed tomatoes
- ½ cup (75 g) pitted Kalamata olives, roughly chopped
- ¼ cup (30 g) capers, drained
- 1 teaspoon dried oregano
- ½ teaspoon red pepper flakes
   Several dashes freshly ground black pepper
- 8 large basil leaves, torn into pieces, plus extra for garnish

For the soft polenta

- 4 cups (960 ml) vegetable broth
- ½ teaspoon salt
- 2 tablespoons olive oil
- 1 cup (120 g) polenta

To assemble

- 2 tablespoons olive oil
- 1 tablespoon fresh lemon juice
- ½ teaspoon flaky sea salt, such as Maldon brand
- 10 ounces (280 g) baby arugula
   Toasted pine nuts for garnish (optional)

Serves 4

1. Make the tofu puttanesca: Preheat a large nonstick heavy-bottomed pan over medium heat. Once the pan is hot, drizzle in 1 tablespoon of the oil. Add the tofu and sprinkle with ¼ teaspoon of the salt. Cook for about 7 minutes, tossing often, until lightly browned on all sides. Transfer to a plate.

2. In the same pan, sauté the garlic in the remaining tablespoon of oil for about 30 seconds, being careful not to burn it. Add the tomatoes, olives, capers, oregano, red pepper flakes, remaining ¼ teaspoon salt, black pepper, and basil leaves and stir. Cover the pot and increase the heat to medium-high. Cook for about 10 minutes to let flavors marry.

3. Return the tofu to the pan and toss to coat and heat through. Turn off the heat and cover to keep warm until ready to use.

4. Make the soft polenta: In a 2-quart (2 L) pot, bring the vegetable broth and salt to a boil. Lower the heat to a simmer and add the oil. Add the polenta in a slow, steady stream, stirring constantly with a whisk. Whisk for about 5 minutes, until the polenta is thickened. Keeping the heat low, cover and let cook for about 20 more minutes, stirring occasionally, until soft and mushy.

5. To assemble: In a medium mixing bowl, mix the oil, lemon juice, and salt. Add the arugula in batches, tossing with your hands to coat. Place a big scoop of polenta in a bowl (ideally a little off to one side). Put the tofu on top, then finish with handfuls of arugula and, if desired, pine nuts and serve.

I Can Cook Vegan

Autumn Everything Bowl with Beet Yogurt Sauce

This is what would happen if autumn spilled its purse into a bowl. Sweet butternut squash, earthy beets, hearty lentils, smoky tempeh bacon, aromatic hazelnuts … enough already—you get it. I love it! Whew. That said, this is definitely a little ambitious in that it requires two million and one pots and pans. But the positive thing is that it will get you two million and two likes on Instagram. Here's the thing, though: it's all about the roasted beet yogurt sauce, so pour that on anything and it becomes an instant autumn bowl! Because this is a multipronged recipe, I suggest only using the lentils and quinoa if you have some left over. If not, try this sauce on quinoa alone or any grain you like! If you roast the butternut squash at the same time as the beets, and make the tempeh bacon while you toast the hazelnuts and steam the kale, everything comes together nicely.

For the roasted beet yogurt sauce

- ½ pound (225 g) beets
- 1 tablespoon chopped fresh ginger
- 2 cups (470 g) unsweetened plain coconut yogurt
- ¼ cup (60 ml) balsamic vinegar

For the butternut squash

- 1 pound (455 g) butternut squash, chopped into medium dice
- 2 tablespoons olive oil

For the steamed kale

- 8 ounces (225 g) kale leaves

To assemble

- 3 cups (605 g) cooked quinoa, warmed
- 2 cups (395 g) cooked lentils, warmed
- 1 recipe Tempeh Bacon (page 68)
- ½ cup (70 g) hazelnuts, toasted

Serves 4

1. Make the roasted beets: Preheat the oven to 400°F (205°C). Wrap the unpeeled whole beets in aluminum foil and place them on a baking sheet. Roast until tender, 45 to 70 minutes, depending on the size of the beets.

2. Make the butternut squash: In the last 20 minutes of roasting the beets, line a large rimmed baking sheet with parchment paper. Toss the butternut with the olive oil and a pinch of salt. Roast for 15 to 20 minutes, tossing once, until tender. Remove from the oven.

3. Make the roasted beet yogurt sauce: Peel the beets when cool enough to touch. Place them in ice water if necessary. In a blender, pulse the ginger to mince. Add the beets, yogurt, and balsamic vinegar and continue to pulse, stopping to scrape the sides of the blender to get everything in, until completely smooth.

4. Make the kale: Set up a steamer. Steam the kale with a pinch of salt for 3 to 5 minutes, until tender.

5. To assemble the bowls, toss together the warmed lentils and quinoa and scoop them into bowls. Add the steamed kale and scatter on the butternut. Top with the tempeh bacon. Drizzle on the roasted beet yogurt sauce and sprinkle with the hazelnuts.

I Can Cook Vegan

Southern Comfort Bowl

This is the absolute easiest way to feel like you went to a chicken place and got everything. Except it's less greasy but still remarkably every bit as good! The tofu is dredged and seasoned in everything delicious, then placed on a pile of cauliflower mashed potatoes, or Caulipots (page 225), and drowned in a white-bean gravy. The collards are more like a slaw, as they are sliced into ribbons and massaged instead of cooked. It's just pure Southern comfort, even if the farthest south I've ever really been is Baltimore. But I promise I know what I'm talking about.

For the tofu

¾ cup (75 g) fine breadcrumbs
1 tablespoon onion powder
1 tablespoon nutritional
      yeast flakes
3 tablespoons tamari or soy sauce
1 (14-ounce/400 g) block
      extra-firm tofu, drained
      and sliced into 8 planks

For the white-bean gravy

1½ cups (360 ml) vegetable
      broth, plus extra for
      thinning, if needed
⅓ cup (40 g) all-purpose flour
2 cloves garlic, chopped
1 tablespoon olive oil
1 teaspoon dried thyme
1 teaspoon dry rubbed sage
      Several dashes freshly
      ground black pepper
1 (15-ounce/425 g) can navy beans,
      drained and rinsed, or 1½ cups
      (275 g) cooked navy beans
2 tablespoons tamari
      Salt

For the collard ribbons

1 tablespoon olive oil
1 tablespoon fresh lemon juice
¼ teaspoon flaky sea salt,
      such as Maldon brand
6 cups (330 g) collard greens
      cut into ribbons, ribs removed

1 recipe Caulipots (page 225)

Recipe continues

I Can Cook Vegan

Serves 4

1. Make the tofu: On a dinner plate, use your fingertips to mix the breadcrumbs, onion powder, and nutritional yeast. Pour the soy sauce onto a separate plate.

2. One at a time, place a tofu slab in the soy sauce and toss to coat. Dredge in the bread-crumb mixture, pressing on both sides of the tofu so it sticks. Be sure to use your dry hand to handle the tofu in the bread-crumbs; otherwise, you'll get a crumb mitten on your hand.

3. Preheat a large nonstick pan, preferably cast-iron, over medium-high heat. Spray the pan with nonstick cooking spray (or put a thin layer of olive oil in the pan) and transfer the tofu planks to the pan. Be careful not to crowd the pan; if it isn't big enough, then cook the tofu in two batches. Spray or brush the tofu with a little oil, cook for a few minutes on the first side, then flip, using a thin metal spatula so you don't scrape off the breading. Continue to cook for about 7 minutes total, spraying more oil or adding a little extra to the pan as needed, flipping occasionally until browned on most sides. When done, cover with aluminum foil to keep warm.

4. Meanwhile, make the cauli-pots according to instructions.

5. Make the gravy: In a meas-uring cup, mix the broth and flour to form a thick slurry. Set aside. Preheat a saucepan over medium heat. Sauté the garlic in the oil for about 30 seconds. Add the thyme, sage, and pepper and cook for about 3 minutes more.

6. If you have an immer-sion blender, add the beans, reserved broth mixture, and tamari to the saucepan. Blend immediately until smooth and lower the heat to medium. Stir the gravy often for about 10 minutes while it thickens. If you are using a regular blender, put the beans, broth mixture, and tamari in the blender and blend until smooth. Transfer the garlic and the other stuff from the pan to the blender. Puree again until no chunks of garlic are left. Return to the pot and stir often over medium heat to thicken. Once the gravy thick-ens, reduce the heat to low. Cook for about 10 minutes more to let the flavors deepen, stirring occasionally. Thin with vegeta-ble broth if it gets too thick. Use salt to taste.

7. Make the collards: Toss everything together in a mixing bowl and rub, rub, rub.

8. Assemble the bowls: Put scoops of caulipots into bowls. Place the collards over the potatoes and place the tofu over that. Smother in gravy and have fun!

Don't sleep on this tofu recipe! Even if you don't want to make the whole bowl, the tofu is worth the price of this book (which is a really affordable book considering how useful it is, but that's another story). I make the tofu a few times a week and throw it into tofu bacon ranch sandwiches (avo, ranch dressing, tomato, mushroom bacon), or onto arugula salads, or with roasted veggies, or to go alongside a stew.

Roasty Couscous Hummus Bowl

You can call it a Mediterranean bowl if you like, but good luck spelling Mediterranean! A mélange of veggies, a bright green chive hummus, and fluffy couscous are sure to satisfy any night of the week. Save some of the chickpea liquid to make the hummus light and fluffy.

For the roasted veggies

1   red bell pepper, sliced into ½-inch-thick (12 mm) pieces
1   Japanese eggplant, sliced into ½-inch-thick (12 mm) half-moons
8   ounces (225 g) cremini mushrooms, sliced in halves
1   medium red onion, quartered and thickly sliced
2   tablespoons olive oil
½   teaspoon salt
    Freshly ground black pepper
1½ cups (240 g) cooked chickpeas

For the fresh chive hummus

1½ cups (240 g) cooked chickpeas (see headnote)
1   clove garlic
¼   cup (60 ml) tahini
3   tablespoons fresh lemon juice
¼   cup (60 ml) olive oil
½   teaspoon salt
½   cup (13 g) chopped fresh chives, plus more for garnish

For the bowl

4   cups (715 g) couscous, cooked according to package directions
4   cups (80 g) loosely packed baby arugula
    A few tablespoons chopped fresh flat-leaf parsley, for garnish

Serves 4

1.   Make the roasted veggies: Preheat the oven to 400°F (205°C).

2.   Line a large rimmed baking sheet with parchment paper. Toss the red pepper, eggplant, mushrooms, and onion with the olive oil, salt, and pepper to taste and spread the veggies in a single layer in the prepared pan. Roast for about 20 minutes and flip them, then roast for another 10 or 15 minutes, until tender and browned. Toss in the chickpeas during the last few minutes to warm them through.

3.   Make the hummus: In a blender or food processor, pulse the chickpeas and garlic to get them chopped. Add the tahini, lemon juice, olive oil, salt, and chives and blend, adding a few tablespoons of the reserved chickpea cooking liquid until the hummus is smooth. The hummus should be just pourable, and not stiff, so you can slather it over everything in the bowl.

4.   To assemble, spoon the couscous into each bowl and top with the arugula and roasted veggies. Serve with the hummus spooned over and extra chives or parsley for garnish.

I Can Cook Vegan

Sushi Bowl with Five-Spice Tempeh

Vegan sushi is about twenty times more exciting than nonvegan. It's not just boring uncooked fish in rice because *zzzzzz*. It's got fun flavors (smokiness! sweetness!), awesome textures (crisp! crunchy!), and adventure galore (hi, carrot ginger dressing)! This sushi bowl reflects that, so go live a little. And don't forget the avocado!

For the tempeh

3 tablespoons tamari
1 tablespoon Sriracha sauce
1 tablespoon sesame oil
1 tablespoon olive oil
1 tablespoon pure maple syrup
1 tablespoon smoked paprika
½ teaspoon five-spice powder
1 (8-ounce/225 g) package tempeh, diced

For the carrot ginger dressing

2 cups (280 g) peeled chopped carrots
2 tablespoons roughly chopped fresh ginger
¼ cup (60 ml) seasoned rice vinegar
1 tablespoon toasted sesame oil
2 tablespoons olive oil
⅛ teaspoon salt

Everything else

4 cups (820 g) sushi rice, cooked according to package directions
4 cups (220 g) loosely packed mixed baby greens
8 ounces (225 g) sugar snap peas, sliced the long way on a bias
2 avocados, peeled, pitted, and sliced
Toasted sesame seeds
1 sheet nori, torn into little pieces
Thinly sliced scallions (white and light green parts only)

Serves 4

1. Make the tempeh: In a mixing bowl, vigorously mix together the tamari, Sriracha, both oils, maple syrup, paprika, and five-spice powder. Add the tempeh and toss to coat. Let marinate for about an hour.

2. Meanwhile, make the dressing: In a blender, combine the carrots, ginger, vinegar, both oils, ½ cup (120 ml) water, and the salt. Puree until relatively smooth.

3. Preheat a large skillet over medium heat. When hot, cook the tempeh for about 10 minutes, flipping often, until caramelized on the edges.

4. To assemble, scoop rice into bowls. Top each serving with a handful of baby greens, cooked tempeh, snap peas, and avocado. Garnish with sesame seeds, nori, and scallions. Serve with the dressing.

I Can Cook Vegan

Portobello Brisket Bowl

As my mother says, brisket is life itself. Portobellos are a fabulous translation for the falling-off-the-bone (falling-off-the-stem?) meatiness of brisket, and the lentil stew supplies that requisite aromatic brothiness, with hints of licorice from fennel and caraway. Mustard greens have just the right bitter and fresh bite to remind me of the Jewish flavors of my youth. I love any version of mashed potatoes here, so follow your heart and get ye to the sides chapter (page 214) to choose!

For the stew

Serves 4

2	cups (230 g) thinly sliced shallots
2	cups (185 g) thinly sliced fennel
2	tablespoons olive oil
2	cloves garlic, minced
1	teaspoon dried thyme
2	bay leaves
1	teaspoon caraway seeds
1	teaspoon salt
	Several dashes freshly ground black pepper
½	cup (95 g) green lentils
1	(25-ounce/710 g) can crushed tomatoes
3	cups (720 ml) vegetable broth

For the portobellos

4	portobello mushrooms, stems removed
¼	cup (60 ml) olive oil
½	teaspoon salt
	Freshly ground black pepper

For the rest of the bowl

1	recipe Caulipots (page 225) or any version of Creamy Mashed Potatoes (page 222)
4	cups (280 g) loosely packed, roughly chopped mustard greens

1. Make the stew: Preheat a 4-quart (3.8 L) pot over medium heat. Sauté the shallots and fennel in the olive oil with a pinch of salt. Add the garlic, thyme, bay leaves, caraway seeds, salt, and pepper and sauté for 1 minute more, until golden and aromatic.

2. Add the lentils, tomatoes, and vegetable broth. Cover the pot and bring to a boil. Continue to cook for about 40 minutes, stirring occasionally, until the lentils are tender.

3. Preheat the oven to 450°F (230°C). Line a rimmed baking sheet with parchment paper. Toss the portobellos with olive oil and sprinkle them with salt and pepper. Arrange the caps on the prepared pan, trimmed side up. Roast until tender and juicy, 18 to 22 minutes.

4. While the mushrooms roast, prepare the caulipots according to directions.

5. To assemble, line bowls with mustard greens. Place scoops of cauliflower mashed potatoes in each bowl and ladle stew over the potatoes. Top each serving with a sliced portobello.

I Can Cook Vegan

Broccoli Goddess Bowl

You are now ready, young bowl maker, for the quintessential bowl. Perhaps even the reason the bowl was invented back in Mesopotamia! Brown rice, the hippiest of tempeh, miso tahini, sprouts, and rainbow carrots will have everyone worshipping at your feet (as they should)!

For the tempeh

1	(8-ounce/225 g) package tempeh, diced
3	tablespoons olive oil
½	teaspoon salt
3	tablespoons nutritional yeast flakes

For the tahini dressing

¼	cup (60 ml) mellow white miso
¼	cup (60 ml) tahini
1	clove garlic

For the rest of the bowl

4	cups (360 g) broccoli florets
4	cups (780 g) cooked brown rice
1	(4-ounce/115 g) package sprouts, such as sunflower, broccoli, alfalfa, or mung bean
2	rainbow carrots, peeled and sliced
1	cup (40 g) loosely packed fresh cilantro leaves, for garnish
4	avocados

Serves 8

1. Make the tempeh: Preheat a large skillet over medium-high heat. Sauté the tempeh in 2 tablespoons of the olive oil with the salt, tossing until browned on all sides, about 10 minutes. Add the remaining tablespoon oil, toss to coat, and shut off the heat. Sprinkle in the nutritional yeast and toss to coat, toasting the yeast a bit. Transfer to a bowl and set aside.

2. Make the dressing: Put the miso, tahini, garlic, and ½ to ¾ cup (120 to 180 ml) water in a blender and blend until completely smooth.

3. Set up a steamer. Steam the broccoli with a pinch or two of salt until tender and bright green, about 7 minutes.

4. To assemble, scoop rice into bowls. To each serving add a pile of sprouts, a pile of tempeh, a pile of carrots, a mound of broccoli, and half of a sliced avocado. Drizzle everything with the tahini dressing and garnish with fresh cilantro.

I Can Cook Vegan

Pantry Mole Bowl with Seitan, Spinach Salad, and Sweet Potatoes

This sauce is such a cheat! There's no way it should have this much depth—smoky and spicy, a little sweet, with a lovely chocolatey undertone. And it only takes seven ingredients instead of the forty-seven you typically associate with mole. The spinach and black bean salad rests on the bottom and is topped with warm, roasted sweet potatoes and grilled seitan that wilt the salad and turn it into something magical by the time you get your first forkful.

For the sweet potatoes

2   pounds (910 g) sweet potatoes, peeled and cut into ¾-inch (2 cm) chunks
2   tablespoons olive oil
½   teaspoon salt

For the pantry mole

1   onion, roughly chopped
1   tablespoon olive oil
    Salt
4   cloves garlic, minced
1   cup (240 ml) vegetable broth
3   chipotles, seeded
½   cup (120 ml) almond butter
1   cup (175 g) chocolate chips
    Additional adobo from canned chipotles

For the seitan

1   pound (455 g) seitan, thinly sliced

For the spinach and black bean salad

4   cups (120 g) fresh spinach
1½   cups (280 g) cooked black beans, or canned, drained and rinsed
1   tablespoon fresh lime juice
1   tablespoon olive oil
    Pinch of salt

    Sliced scallions (white and light green parts only), for garnish

Recipe continues

I Can Cook Vegan

Serves 4

1. Make the sweet potatoes: Preheat the oven to 450°F (230°C). Line a rimmed baking sheet with parchment paper.

2. Toss the potatoes, oil, and salt on the baking sheet. Roast for 30 minutes, tossing once, until lightly browned and tender inside.

3. Make the pantry mole: Preheat a saucepan over medium heat. Sauté onion in the oil with a pinch of salt for 5 to 7 minutes, until lightly golden. Add the garlic and sauté until fragrant, about 30 seconds.

4. Add the broth and turn the heat up to warm the liquid. Add the chipotles, almond butter, chocolate chips, and ½ teaspoon salt. Whisk together to melt the chocolate.

5. Lower heat and use an immersion blender to blend the chocolate mixture smooth. You can also transfer the mixture to a blender and puree. Add the adobo sauce to taste, a scant tablespoon at a time. Keep the mole warm until ready to serve.

6. Make the seitan: Preheat a cast-iron grill pan over medium heat. Spray with nonstick cooking spray. Grill seitan on each side until grill marks appear, about 3 minutes.

7. Make the spinach and black bean salad: Toss all ingredients together in a mixing bowl.

8. To assemble, place a handful of spinach and black bean salad at the bottom of each bowl. Add a layer of sweet potatoes and then a layer of seitan. Douse in mole. Garnish with the sliced scallions.

If you don't want to be awake at 1 A.M. googling "how to get your hands to stop burning from touching chipotles," then listen to me: Wear gloves or plastic bags on your hands when removing the seeds from the chipotles. Because what your google search will turn up is not pretty.

Scrambly Tofu with Mushrooms, Spinach, and Red Pepper

Obviously, scrambled tofu makes for a great breakfast; but have you ever considered having it for breakfast, lunch, dinner, and a midnight snack? What I'm saying is that it's fast, convenient, and yummy as heck any time of day. And I probably make it more times a week than I can count. If you've never made it before, the idea is to get the tofu nice and seared but still moist and mouthwatering. The texture should resemble scrambled eggs but about a thousand times better.

Ingredients

Serves 4

1 large red bell pepper, diced small
3 tablespoons olive oil
3 cloves garlic, minced
8 ounces (225 g) cremini mushrooms, thinly sliced
1 (14-ounce/400 g) package extra-firm tofu, drained
1 teaspoon salt, plus more to taste
   Freshly ground black pepper
1 tablespoon onion powder
½ teaspoon ground turmeric
¼ cup (15 g) nutritional yeast flakes
4 cups (120 g) fresh spinach

1.   Preheat a large heavy-bottomed pan over medium-high heat. Sauté the red pepper in 1 tablespoon of the olive oil for about 5 minutes, until softened. Mix in the garlic. Add mushrooms and toss to coat. Cook for about 3 minutes, until some of the moisture has released.

2.   Break apart the tofu into bite-size pieces and stir into the pan. Drizzle with the remaining 2 tablespoons olive oil, the salt, and pepper to taste. Cook for about 10 minutes, stirring often with a thin spatula. Get under the tofu when you are stirring; scrape the bottom of the pan and don't let the tofu stick to the pan—that is where the good crispy stuff is.

3.   Drizzle in ¼ cup (60 ml) water. Sprinkle the onion powder and turmeric on the tofu and mix so that the turmeric colors the tofu. Add the nutritional yeast to coat. Cook for 3 minutes.

4.   Add the spinach and toss until it starts to wilt. If you need a little extra water, go for it. Taste for salt and pepper and serve!

Chapter

6

From
the
Oven

Mission: Let's get homey! Learn to infuse vegan proteins with loads of flavor and make your friends say things like "I'd go vegan if everything tasted like this!"

Do you want to do the whole 1950s housewife thing: wear oven mitts and smile at your casserole? Then this chapter is for you! No big secret here, it's in the title … this is stuff you make in the oven! Some are casseroles and some of these dishes are roasted with a separate sauce, but the beauty of this chapter is that wonderful bakiness that reminds you how warm and cozy cooking can be.

Equipment must-haves

Large rimmed baking sheets
Cast-iron skillet
Really excellent oven mitts
    (preferably shaped like cats)

You might also notice how meaty these recipes are, but this isn't about "fake" meats. Or maybe it is. I like to think of these as translations of traditionally meaty dishes that use beans, vegetables, grains, and the like, instead of, you know, gross meat. There's lots of finger-wagging at vegan chefs for trying to imitate meat, but I promise, that's not what I'm doing. I'm saying, hey, that was a great flavor combo, or hmm, that's a texture I miss, or even, ha, this tastes better vegan, so bully to me! Anyway, it doesn't have to be tofu, tempeh, or seitan to be meaty—it just has to be hearty and satisfying. That said, using tofu, tempeh, or seitan doesn't hurt.

From the Oven

Baked Tofu with Peanut Sauce and Bok Choy

Peanut, sesame, and tamari are classic craveable flavors, and baking the bok choy gives it a fun, unexpected texture. The thick stems are tender but still crunchy and juicy, and the leaves are wilted and a little crisp in places. This peanut sauce is great because there is no cooking required and it uses very few ingredients. Make a triple batch because you'll want to drizzle it on everything from salad to baked sweet potatoes.

For the tofu and bok choy

2	(14-ounce/400 g) packages extra-firm tofu, drained, each sliced into 8 planks
2	tablespoons toasted sesame oil
1	tablespoon tamari or soy sauce
	Freshly ground black pepper
3	heads baby bok choy, stems removed, leaves separated
	Salt

For the peanut sauce

½	cup (135 g) smooth natural peanut butter
¼	teaspoon salt
¼	cup (60 ml) fresh lime juice
1	tablespoon chopped fresh ginger
¼	cup (60 ml) hoisin sauce
½	teaspoon red pepper flakes

For garnish

½	cup (50 g) thinly sliced scallions (white and light green parts only)
	Red pepper flakes (optional)

Serves 4 to 6

1. Make the tofu: Preheat the oven to 350°F (175°C). Place the tofu on a large rimmed baking sheet and drizzle with 1 tablespoon of the sesame oil and the tamari, flipping the planks to make sure they're well coated. Sprinkle with black pepper. Arrange the tofu slices in a single layer. Cover tightly with aluminum foil and bake for 20 minutes.

2. Remove the foil and flip the tofu slices, pushing them to one side. Add the bok choy and drizzle with the remaining sesame oil. Sprinkle with a little salt. Bake for 15 minutes, uncovered, until the tofu is browned on the edges and the bok choy is wilted.

3. While the tofu is finishing, make the peanut sauce: In a blender, combine the peanut butter, ½ cup (120 ml) water, salt, lime juice, ginger, hoisin sauce, and red pepper flakes and blend until smooth. Use additional water to thin the sauce, if necessary.

4. To assemble, divide the tofu and bok choy among plates. Drizzle with peanut sauce and garnish with scallions and red pepper flakes, if desired.

I Can Cook Vegan

Lemon Yuba and Rice

If you're not familiar with yuba, now is the time to get acquainted because it's gaining in popularity here in the USA. Often referred to as "tofu skin," yuba features layers of chewy, crispy goodness that echo the flakiness of chicken, but guess what?—it's plants! And I love it. Every time I make this rice I feel like someone else cooked for me because how in the world did I make something so wonderful? Inspired by baked chicken and rice, it's definitely "last meal" material. Hint: You absolutely need a cast-iron pan for this. And you'll want an audience when you pull it out of the oven because it's that glorious. If you can't find yuba, then slice half a block of extra-firm tofu as thinly as you can get it. It's not quite the same, but it's a decent replacement.

For the yuba

1   tablespoon olive oil
1   teaspoon grated lemon zest
    Freshly ground black pepper
1   (8-ounce/225 g) package yuba

For the rice

1   medium yellow onion,
        finely chopped
¼   cup (35 g) thinly sliced garlic
2   tablespoons olive oil
2   teaspoons dried oregano
½   teaspoon salt
    Freshly ground black pepper
3½ cups (840 ml) vegetable broth
½   teaspoon ground turmeric
¼   cup (60 ml) fresh lemon juice
2   teaspoons grated lemon zest
1½ cups (285 g) white jasmine rice

For baking and garnish

6   to 8 thin slices of lemon
    Finely chopped fresh
        flat-leaf parsley

Serves 4 to 6

1.   Prepare the yuba: Mix together the olive oil, lemon zest, and black pepper to taste in a wide shallow bowl. Add the yuba, layers separated, and toss to coat.

2.   Preheat a large cast-iron skillet over medium heat. Lightly spray it with nonstick cooking spray. Add the yuba with its dressing to the pan and sauté for about 5 minutes, until the yuba is very lightly browned. Transfer back to the bowl.

3.   Make the rice: Preheat the oven to 350°F (175°C). In the same cast-iron pan over medium heat, sauté the onion and garlic in the olive oil for about 5 minutes. Add the oregano, salt, and black pepper to taste and toss to coat. Then add the broth, turmeric, lemon juice, and lemon zest. Mix in the rice. Scatter the yuba over the top of the vegetable mixture, leaving some room around the edges of the pan. Place the lemon slices over the yuba.

4.   Cover the pan and bake for about 40 minutes, until the rice is cooked. The cast-iron will be very hot, so use oven mitts and be careful when removing it from the oven. Uncover carefully (because there will be lots of hot steam) and sprinkle with parsley. Serve!

I Can Cook Vegan

Green Enchilada Lasagna

Layers of fragrant salsa verde, juicy summer squash, and meaty black beans—now that's a casserole! It's a little more work than some of the other recipes in this book, but it's easier if you buy the salsa verde and still not too complicated if you make it yourself. The most fun task is undressing the green tomatillos from their papery husks. This is definitely potluck fare.

For the filling

Serves 8

1	onion, quartered and thinly sliced
2	tablespoons olive oil
2	cloves garlic, minced
2	medium yellow squash, cut into ¼-inch-thick (6 mm) half-moons (3 cups/345 g)
2	teaspoons ground cumin
½	teaspoon salt
3	cups (555 g) cooked black beans, or two 15-ounce (425 g) cans, drained and rinsed

For the queso sauce

1	cup (120 g) whole unroasted cashews (if you don't own a high-speed blender, see page 24)
½	teaspoon salt
2	teaspoons cornstarch
1	teaspoon ground cumin
1	recipe Salsa Verde (page 194)
18	(8-inch/20 cm) corn tortillas
1	cup (240 ml) Pico de Gallo (page 66)
½	cup (20 g) chopped fresh cilantro leaves

1. Make the filling: Preheat a large pan over medium heat. Sauté the onion in the oil with a pinch of salt for about 5 minutes, until translucent. Add the garlic and sauté just until fragrant, 30 seconds or so. Add the squash, cumin, and salt and cook until the squash have released a lot of their moisture, about 5 minutes. Add the beans and cook just until heated through, 2 minutes or so.

2. Make the queso: Add all the ingredients plus ¾ cup (180 ml) water to a blender and puree until completely smooth. The sauce is rather thick, so scrape the sides with a rubber spatula often to make sure you get everything.

3. Preheat the oven to 350°F (175°C) and lightly grease a 9 by 13-inch (23 by 33 cm) casserole dish.

4. To assemble the casserole, ladle a thin layer of salsa verde to cover the bottom of the pan, then add 6 of the tortillas. Ladle in another layer of salsa verde (about 1 cup/240 ml) and flip each tortilla to smother them in the sauce. Arrange the tortillas so they're slightly overlapping and covering the bottom of the pan.

5. Add half the filling and pour ½ cup (120 ml) of the salsa on top. Layer in 6 more tortillas and repeat the process of smothering each of them in a cup of salsa. Cover with the remaining filling. Pour ½ cup (120 ml) of salsa verde over the filling and add the final layer of tortillas. Smother those in the remaining salsa verde. Spoon the queso sauce in ribbons over the top.

6. Bake the casserole for about 30 minutes. The topping should be lightly golden. Remove from the oven and top with pico de gallo and fresh cilantro leaves before serving.

I Can Cook Vegan

Salsa Verde

Ingredients

3 cloves garlic, minced
2 jalapeños, thinly sliced
2 tablespoons olive oil
2 pounds (910 g) tomatillos,
   husked and diced
½ teaspoon salt
3 cups (720 ml) vegetable broth
1 cup (40 g) loosely packed
   fresh cilantro
1 tablespoon fresh lime juice

Makes 6 cups (1.4 L)

1.   Preheat a 4-quart (3.8 L) pot over medium-low heat. Sauté the garlic and jalapeños in the oil for about 3 minutes.

2.   Add the tomatillos and salt, raise the heat to medium-high, and sauté until the tomatillos begin to soften and release moisture, about 5 minutes.

3.   Pour in the vegetable broth, bring to a slow boil, and continue to boil for about 20 minutes, stirring occasionally.

4.   Remove from the heat, let cool until the salsa stops steaming, then add the cilantro and lime juice. Pour into a blender and blend until relatively smooth.

Don't wanna unhusk and chop a bunch of tomatillos no matter how fun I insist it is? I hear you! You can replace the fresh tomatillos with two 15-ounce (430 g) cans of tomatillos. You can reduce the cooking time by 15 minutes as well. You're welcome.

Your First Vegan Lasagna

If you've never made a vegan lasagna, this is where to start. Tofu ricotta, garlicky spinach and mushrooms, and bursts of Kalamata olives . . . it's so saucy that there's no need to precook the noodles because they'll cook right there in the casserole. Packed with flavor, so so easy, and possibly even better as leftovers. I love it with a Caesar salad (page 64).

For the spinach and mushroom filling

4   cloves garlic
2   tablespoons olive oil
1   pound (455 g) cremini
     mushrooms, thinly sliced
2   tablespoons fresh thyme leaves
1   cup (155 g) pitted Kalamata
     olives, sliced in half
1   (16-ounce/455 g) bag
     baby spinach

For the tofu ricotta

2   (14-ounce/400 g) blocks
     extra-firm tofu, crumbled
¼   cup (35 g) nutritional yeast flakes
2   tablespoons olive oil
2   tablespoons fresh lemon juice
1   teaspoon salt
     Freshly ground black pepper

8   cups (2 L) marinara
     sauce, store-bought or
     homemade (page 278)
1   (14-ounce/400 g) box
     lasagna noodles
2   cups (200 g) breadcrumbs
2   tablespoons olive oil
2   tablespoons chopped fresh
     thyme or fresh flat-leaf
     parsley, for garnish (optional)

Serves 8 to 10

1.   Make the filling: Preheat a large pan over medium heat. Sauté the garlic in olive oil for about 30 seconds. Turn up the heat, add the mushrooms and thyme, and sauté until lightly browned, about 7 minutes.

2.   Toss in the olives. Turn off the heat and add the spinach in handfuls, tossing it until wilted. This might take a few rounds. Set the filling aside.

3.   Make the ricotta: Using your hands (or an avocado masher), mash the tofu until it resembles ricotta. Add the nutritional yeast, olive oil, lemon juice, salt, and pepper to taste and continue to mash until well combined.

4.   Preheat the oven to 375°F (190°C). Lightly grease the bottom of the casserole dish with olive oil. Ladle in a thin layer of marinara, then arrange a single layer of uncooked noodles over the sauce. Ladle in another layer of sauce that is about ½ inch (12 mm) deep. Then arrange half of the filling on top of that and spoon in half of the ricotta in scattered dollops. Over the ricotta, ladle in another ½-inch (12 mm) layer of sauce, then repeat layers of the noodles, mushroom filling, ricotta, sauce, and another layer of noodles. That will be the top layer.

5.   Ladle plenty of marinara sauce over the top layer. Tightly seal the lasagna in aluminum foil and bake for about an hour. In the meantime, mix the breadcrumbs with the olive oil in a mixing bowl.

6.   Once the noodles are tender, remove the foil. Scatter the breadcrumbs over the top and bake, uncovered, for an additional 20 minutes. Garnish the lasagna with fresh thyme or parsley, if desired, and serve!

I Can Cook Vegan

Cheezy Broccoli Bake

Sometimes nothing but broccoli and cheese will do! This is one of those Americana-style recipes you'd find in a recipe box at a thrift store, only Granny didn't use quite as much nutritional yeast. If you would rather use fresh broccoli, just steam it for five minutes first.

Ingredients

Serves 6 to 8

- 1 large onion, chopped into medium dice
- 2 tablespoons olive oil
- 4 cloves garlic, minced
- 1 (16-ounce/450 g) package frozen broccoli
- 1 (12-ounce/340 g) package extra-firm silken tofu (the vacuum-packed kind)
- ½ cup (120 ml) vegetable broth
- ½ cup (120 ml) tahini
- ¼ cup (60 ml) fresh lemon juice
- 1 teaspoon sweet paprika, plus more for garnish
- ¼ cup (35 g) nutritional yeast flakes
- 1 teaspoon ground turmeric
- ½ teaspoon salt
  Several dashes freshly ground black pepper
- 1 cup (100 g) breadcrumbs

1. Preheat a large pan over medium heat. Sauté the onion in the olive oil with a pinch of salt until translucent, about 5 minutes. Add the garlic and sauté for another minute. Add the broccoli, raise the heat a bit, and cook until the broccoli is thawed.

2. Preheat the oven to 350°F (175°C). Lightly grease a 10 by 10-inch (25 by 25 cm) casserole dish. In a food processor, combine the tofu, vegetable broth, tahini, and lemon juice and blend until completely smooth. Add half of the broccoli mixture, the paprika, nutritional yeast, salt, and pepper and pulse a few times until well combined. Without running the food processor, stir in the breadcrumbs with a spatula. I do this just to save a dish, but you can transfer to a mixing bowl to stir in the breadcrumbs there if you prefer. You just don't want to food process them at this point because it would make the dish gummy.

3. Transfer the mixture from the food processor to the casserole and spread it out evenly. Top with the remaining broccoli mixture and lightly press it into the bottom layer.

4. Bake for 30 minutes, until golden on top. Let cool slightly, sprinkle with additional paprika, and serve!

I Can Cook Vegan

Lentil and Mushroom Shepherd's Pie

Is there anything more comforting than mashed potatoes and stew all baked together in one gorgeous casserole? Of course not. The potatoes are golden and browned on top. Poke your fork in and inside is a juicy concoction of lentils, mushrooms, and veggies. Meat-and-potatoes heaven in one piping hot dish.

Ingredients

Serves 8

2 cups (480 ml) cold vegetable broth
1 tablespoon cornstarch
2 tablespoons tomato paste
1 yellow onion, chopped into medium dice
2 medium carrots, thinly sliced into half-moons
2 tablespoons olive oil
2 cloves garlic, minced
2 ribs celery, thinly sliced
1 pound (450 g) cremini mushrooms, chopped into pea-size pieces
3 tablespoons fresh thyme
  Freshly ground black pepper
1 teaspoon salt
4 cups (790 g) cooked lentils
1 cup (135 g) frozen peas
1 recipe Classic Mashed Potatoes (page 222)
  Chopped fresh flat-leaf parsley, for garnish (optional)

1.   In a measuring cup, mix together the broth and cornstarch until the starch is mostly dissolved. Mix in the tomato paste and set aside.

2.   Preheat a large pan over medium heat. Sauté the onion and carrots in the olive oil with a pinch of salt until the onions are lightly browned, 5 to 7 minutes. Add the garlic and sauté for 30 seconds or so, just until fragrant. Add the celery, mushrooms, and thyme with a bunch of fresh black pepper and the salt. Let cook for about 5 minutes, until the mushrooms have released a lot of moisture.

3.   Add the lentils and use your spatula to mush them in the pan to create a "ground beef" effect. Add the cornstarch-broth mixture and mix well. Let cook until the filling is thick and gravy-like, about 7 minutes. Fold in the peas. Taste for salt and seasoning.

4.   Preheat the oven to 350°F (175°C). Lightly grease an 11 by 13-inch (28 by 33 cm) casserole dish. Transfer the filling to the casserole in an even layer. Dollop the mashed potatoes over the top, starting at the edges and working your way in, and then use a rubber spatula to spread them relatively smoothly.

5.   Place the casserole dish on a baking sheet to collect any juices that bubble over. Bake for 25 to 30 minutes, until the potatoes are browned. Let cool a bit before sprinkling with parsley, if desired, and serving.

I Can Cook Vegan

Swedish Tofu Balls

Okay, confession time . . . I went vegan way before I had a chance to try authentic Swedish meatballs, so the ones I knew and loved came from a microwave dinner. But I won't lie: They were my favorite meal of all time! I've tried to re-create the magic here with light, savory balls, made with tofu for chewiness and tahini for depth. The gravy is rich, creamy, and funky, just like I remember it. And I guess I am going to get booed out of Sweden when I say that cranberry sauce is fantabulous with these, too, if you can't find the traditional lingonberry jam. Serve over pasta or mashed potatoes!

For the gravy

3   cups (720 ml) vegetable broth
1   cup (120 g) whole unroasted cashews (if you don't own a high-speed blender, see page 24)
¼   cup (8 g) dried porcini mushrooms
½   teaspoon salt
⅛   teaspoon ground white pepper

For the balls

1   (14-ounce/400 g) package extra-firm tofu
1   small onion, very finely chopped
3   tablespoons soy sauce
3   tablespoons tahini
½   cup (100 g) breadcrumbs
⅓   cup (40 g) all-purpose flour
    Olive oil, for pan-frying

    Lingonberry jam and cranberry sauce, for serving
    Chopped fresh flat-leaf parsley, for garnish

Serves 6

1. Make the gravy: Combine all the ingredients in a high-speed blender. Blend until very smooth, occasionally scraping the sides with a rubber spatula. Transfer to a small pot and gently heat until thick and bubbly. Cover and set aside.

2. Make the balls: In a medium mixing bowl, using your hands (or an avocado masher), mash the tofu until it resembles ricotta. Mix in the onion, soy sauce, tahini, and breadcrumbs until they are firm and hold together easily.

3. Pour the flour into a wide shallow bowl or a rimmed dinner plate. Roll the tofu mixture into 14 to 16 golf ball–size balls. Roll each ball in the flour.

4. Preheat a large skillet over medium heat. Pour a thin layer of olive oil into the skillet. Drop in a little flour and if it bubbles quickly, the oil is ready. Fry the balls in batches, turning them occasionally until browned on all sides, about 5 minutes per batch.

5. Serve over pasta or mashed potatoes with gravy and dollops of lingonberry jam or cranberry sauce. Garnish with parsley.

I Can Cook Vegan

Sunday Night Lentil Roast

This is the roast to end all roasts (and the perfect Sunday night centerpiece)! Serve with any of the fabulous potatoes that you will learn to make (see On the Side, pages 214–230) and some steamed or roasted veggies. The flavors are really versatile, so if you'd like to add a sauce, try serving it with mushroom gravy (page 202), White-Bean Gravy (page 164), or Marinara (page 278; pictured on opposite page). This roast is not complicated to make, so don't assume that because it looks so professional it's out of reach. You puree some stuff, mix it in a bowl, and wrap it in aluminum foil. Give it a try!

Ingredients

Serves 6 to 8

3   cloves garlic
¾   cup (150 g) cooked brown or green lentils, or canned, drained and rinsed
1½   (360 ml) cups vegetable broth
3   tablespoons tomato paste
¼   cup (60 ml) tamari or soy sauce
3   tablespoons olive oil
2   cups (305 g) vital wheat gluten
⅓   cup (50 g) nutritional yeast flakes
1   tablespoon onion powder
1   teaspoon smoked paprika
½   teaspoon dried thyme, crushed between your fingers
        Several dashes freshly ground black pepper

1. Preheat the oven to 350°F (175°C). Spread out a large rectangular sheet of aluminum foil that is at least 16 inches (40.5 cm) long.

2. In a food processor, pulse the garlic until well chopped. Add the lentils, broth, tomato paste, tamari, and olive oil and puree until relatively smooth.

3. In a large mixing bowl, mix the wheat gluten, nutritional yeast, onion powder, paprika, thyme, and black pepper. Make a well in the center and add the lentil mixture. Stir with a wooden spoon until the mixture starts coming together to form a ball of dough. Knead until everything is well incorporated.

4. Shape the mixture into a log that is roughly 8 inches (20 cm) long. The log doesn't have to be perfectly formed because the shape will adjust itself as it bakes.

5. Place the log lengthwise in the center of the foil and roll it up like a Tootsie Roll, making sure the ends are tightly wrapped. Transfer to a baking sheet and bake for 1 hour and 15 minutes. Rotate the roll every 20 minutes for even cooking.

6. Once the roast is cooked through, let cool until it's not too hot to handle. Slice into ¾-inch-thick (2 cm) pieces and serve.

I Can Cook Vegan

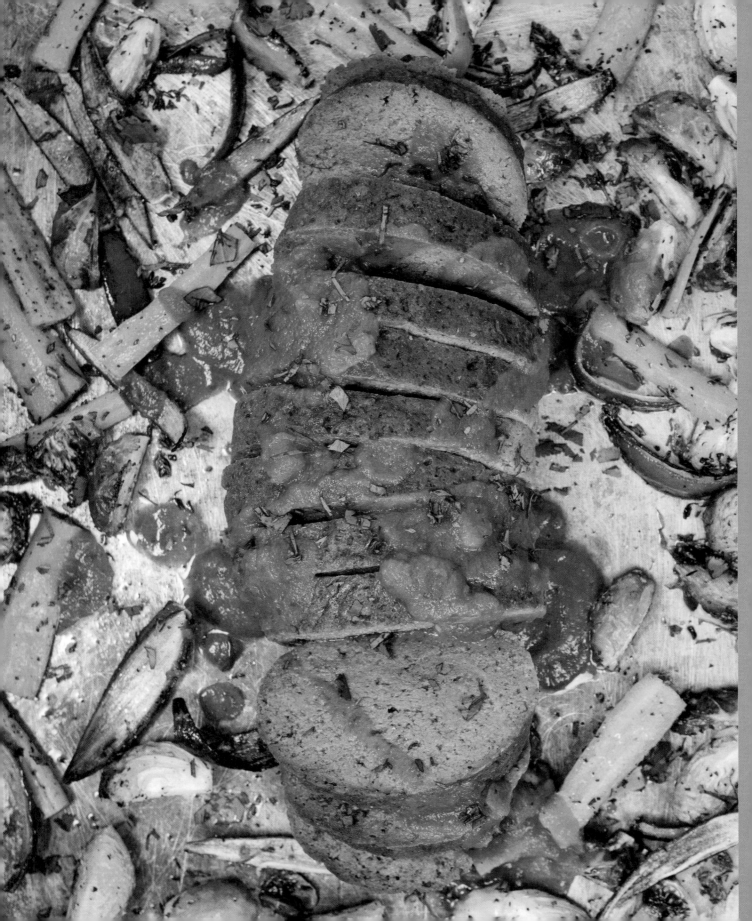

Tofu Fish Sticks with Tartar Sauce

Juicy lemony tofu with crunchy coating, dipped in tartar sauce—who needs to destroy our oceans for fish? Not us humans. This takes a few plates and a little bit of attention to detail, so don't save this for a speedy weeknight dinner. Instead, set aside an hour or so on a Sunday night to make this special treat.

For the tofu fish sticks

Serves 4 to 6

2	(14-ounce/400 g) packages extra-firm tofu, drained and pressed (see page 26)
2	tablespoons tamari
1	tablespoon fresh lemon juice
1	tablespoon fresh nori or kelp powder, plus extra for garnish (optional)
½	cup (65 g) plus 2 tablespoons all-purpose flour
2	tablespoons cornstarch
1	cup (240 ml) cold water
1	cup (80 g) panko breadcrumbs
1	teaspoon kosher salt
2	tablespoons olive oil
	Chopped fresh flat-leaf parsley, for garnish

For the tartar sauce

1	cup (240 ml) vegan mayonnaise, store-bought or homemade (page 277)
⅓	cup (50 g) finely chopped dill pickles
¼	cup (35 g) minced yellow onion
1	tablespoon chopped fresh flat-leaf parsley
1	tablespoon fresh lemon juice
1	teaspoon whole-grain Dijon mustard
2	tablespoons drained and chopped capers
	Freshly ground black pepper

1. Preheat the oven to 450°F (230°C). Line a large rimmed baking sheet with parchment paper and spray with nonstick cooking spray. Slice each block of tofu into 16 sticks. Have ready two dinner plates and a wide shallow bowl.

2. On one of the plates, mix the tamari, lemon juice, and nori powder.

3. In the bowl, toss the flour and cornstarch. Add the water and stir vigorously with a fork to make a thick, smooth batter.

4. On the other plate, mix the breadcrumbs and salt. Drizzle in the oil and use your fingertips to coat the breadcrumbs.

5. One at a time, dredge a tofu stick in the tamari mixture, then into the batter, and let the excess drip off. Transfer to the breadcrumbs plate and use the other (dry) hand to sprinkle a handful of breadcrumbs over it to coat completely. Gently press breadcrumbs into the tofu to help them stick. Transfer the tofu to the prepared baking sheet and repeat with the remaining tofu sticks.

6. Bake tofu sticks for 10 minutes. Flip and bake for another 8 to 10 minutes. The sticks should be crisp and varying shades of brown. Taste one to check for doneness.

7. Mix together the tartar sauce ingredients. Serve the fish sticks as soon as possible with the tartar sauce. Sprinkle them with extra nori powder, if you like, and some fresh parsley, too.

BBQ Tempeh Ribs

Smoky, sticky, sweet, finger-licking ribs! (Just be sure to lick YOUR OWN fingers.) These are inspired by Homegrown Smoker, my fave vegan BBQ joint in Portland, Oregon. I'm not saying my ribs are as good, but they get me there without the airfare. Serve with corn or mashed potatoes or mashed sweet potatoes or rice or coleslaw or all of the above.

For the BBQ sauce

2	tablespoons cornstarch
1	cup (240 ml) cold vegetable broth
1¼	cups (300 ml) ketchup
⅓	cup packed (75 g) brown sugar
⅓	cup (75 ml) tamari or soy sauce
⅓	cup (75 ml) apple cider vinegar
2	teaspoons liquid smoke
1½	tablespoons garlic powder
1	tablespoon onion powder
¼	teaspoon cayenne

For the ribs

2	tablespoons olive oil
2	(8-ounce/225 g) packages tempeh, sliced widthwise into 8 pieces

Serves 4

1. Make the sauce: In a saucepot, use a fork to vigorously whisk the cornstarch into the vegetable broth until it's mostly dissolved. Add the remaining ingredients and mix well. Place over medium heat, stirring occasionally, until the mixture comes to a boil. Once boiling, lower the heat to a low simmer and let the sauce thicken for about 5 minutes. Remove from the heat.

2. Make the ribs: Preheat a large skillet over medium heat. Drizzle in 1 tablespoon of the oil and a pinch of salt. Fry the tempeh pieces on one side until browned, about 5 minutes. Drizzle the remaining oil over the tempeh and sprinkle with salt, then flip and brown the other side.

3. Pour about ½ cup (120 ml) of the barbeque sauce into the pan and toss the tempeh to coat. Let the tempeh cook and caramelize for about 3 minutes.

4. Transfer the tempeh to a platter or plates and serve with more barbeque sauce drizzled over.

I Can Cook Vegan

Sun-Dried Tomato and Spinach Frittata

A frittata is a baked omelet, essentially. This one is made with chickpea flour, which tastes unreasonably eggy! Just perfect for when your soy-free friend wants brunch, or you just want something to pull out of the oven for dinner with little to no fuss. You can absolutely switch up the flavors: try kale or broccoli instead of the spinach; olives or roasted red peppers instead of the sun-dried tomatoes. This frittata is your canvas!

Ingredients

Serves 6 to 8

1   large onion, diced
3   tablespoons olive oil
      Salt
2   cloves garlic, minced
6   cups (180 g) fresh spinach leaves
½   cup (55 g) sun-dried
        tomatoes in oil, chopped
1   teaspoon ground turmeric
2   cups (480 ml) vegetable broth
2   cups (185 g) chickpea flour

1.   Preheat the oven to 350°F (175°C). Lightly grease a 10 by 10-inch (25 by 25 cm) casserole dish.

2.   Preheat a large pan over medium heat. Sauté onion in 1 tablespoon of the olive oil with a pinch of salt until translucent, about 5 minutes. Add the garlic and sauté for another minute. Add the spinach and cook just until wilted. Stir in the sun-dried tomatoes, ¾ teaspoon salt, and turmeric and turn off the heat.

3.   Add the vegetable broth and remaining 2 tablespoons oil and then slowly sprinkle in the chickpea flour, stirring constantly, until the flour is all absorbed and a thick batter is formed.

4.   Transfer the mixture to the prepared casserole dish and spread it out evenly. Bake for 25 to 28 minutes, until golden and firm on top but slightly jiggly in the middle—that means it's not dried out. Let cool slightly, slice, and serve!

I Can Cook Vegan

Chapter

7

On the
Side

Mission: Just a few go-to recipes that are pretty much the little black dress of "What should I serve with that?"

Side dishes are a social construct. I mean, really, the side dish is a relic, especially for vegan cooking, where you have what is traditionally considered a "side"—beans, veggies, grains— now functioning as the main event. But there are a few classic sides that I turn to ALL THE TIME and that you will definitely need in your life. Most of them feature potatoes. You can find them in this chapter!

I Can Cook Vegan

On the Side

Potatoes au Gratin

"Au gratin" is French for "sprinkle me with cheese and breadcrumbs, by golly." So you better do it. Layers of thinly sliced golden potatoes are baked in a creamy, cheesy casserole with some breadcrumbs sprinkled on top for extra crunch and toastiness. It's a bit more fussy than mashed potatoes, but these are so worth it when you feel like fussing. They're also perfect for potlucks, Thanksgivings, or anywhere potato fans are gathered.

Ingredients

- 1 cup (120 g) whole unroasted cashews (if you don't own a high-speed blender, see page 24)
- ¼ cup (35 g) nutritional yeast flakes
- 2 cups (480 ml) vegetable broth
- 1 medium yellow onion, thinly sliced
- 2 tablespoons olive oil
- ½ cup (60 g) breadcrumbs
- 2 tablespoons fresh lemon juice
- Freshly ground black pepper
- ¾ teaspoon salt
- 3 pounds (1.4 kg) russet potatoes (about 4 large), peeled and sliced ⅛ inch (3 mm) thick
- Big handful chopped fresh flat-leaf parsley, for garnish (optional)

Serves 6 to 8

1. Preheat the oven to 400°F (205°C). In a high-speed blender, combine the cashews, nutritional yeast, and broth. Blend until very smooth, scraping down the sides with a rubber spatula occasionally.

2. Preheat a large pan over medium heat. Sauté the onion in the oil, along with a dash of salt, until nice and brown, 7 to 10 minutes. Add ¼ cup (25 g) of the breadcrumbs and toss to coat the onions. Continue to cook until the breadcrumbs turn a few shades darker, about 3 minutes.

3. Pour the cashew mixture into the pan and lower the heat a bit. Add the lemon juice, several dashes of pepper, and the salt and mix well. Let cook for 2 minutes (the sauce should begin to thicken). Taste for salt and adjust the seasoning if needed.

4. Lightly spray a 2-quart (9 by 13-inch/23 by 33 cm) casserole dish or cast-iron pan with nonstick cooking spray (or lightly grease it with olive oil). Pour half of the sauce into the casserole. Arrange the potato slices in the casserole in slightly overlapping layers, dredging the potatoes in the sauce as you layer.

5. Pour the remaining sauce over the potatoes. Use a rubber spatula to spread the sauce if needed (they should be mostly submerged). Sprinkle with the remaining ¼ cup (25 g) breadcrumbs and spray the top with cooking spray.

6. Seal tightly with aluminum foil and bake for about 40 minutes, or until the potatoes are easily pierced with a fork. Remove the foil and bake for an additional 20 to 30 minutes, until the the top is nice and brown. Sprinkle with parsley to serve, if desired.

Hasselback Potatoes

If you've ever looked at Pinterest, or a cookbook from the 1970s, you've seen these. But unlike other food trends, like, say, unicorn ice cream, hasselback potatoes are totally worth making. They're like a row of potato chips growing off a French fry!

Ingredients

Serves 4

¼ cup (60 ml) olive oil
1 teaspoon paprika
1 teaspoon salt
   Freshly ground black pepper
4 large russet potatoes
¼ cup (13 g) thinly sliced chives

1. Preheat the oven to 425°F (220°C). Line a small roasting pan or rimmed baking sheet with parchment paper. In a small cup, mix the olive oil, paprika, salt, and a big pinch of pepper.

2. Use a large, sharp knife to cut the potato crosswise into about ⅛-inch (3 mm) slices, keeping the bottom of the potato intact.

3. Place the potatoes cut side up on the prepared pan. Drizzle with 2 tablespoons of the olive oil mixture.

4. Bake for about 40 minutes, until the slices are separated and lightly browned on the edges. Remove from the oven and drizzle with the rest of the olive oil mixture. Bake for another 20 minutes or so, until crispy and brown. Sprinkle with chives when ready to serve.

I Can Cook Vegan

Creamy Mashed Potatoes, Three or Four Ways

These are the creamiest mashed potatoes going. And if you've even glanced my way, you know how they get there: cashews and coconut oil! Because one mashed potato recipe would be underachieving, I offer you three versions . . . or four if you're counting regular ol' mashed taters!

Classic mashed potatoes

2½ pounds (1.2 kg) russet potatoes, peeled and cut into 1½-inch (4 cm) chunks
2¾ teaspoons salt
⅓ cup (40 g) whole unroasted cashews (if you don't own a high-speed blender, see page 24)
½ cup (120 ml) vegetable broth, at room temperature
⅓ cup (75 ml) refined coconut oil, at room temperature
Freshly ground black pepper

Serves 4

1. Place the potatoes in a pot and add enough cold water to submerge them by about an inch (2.5 cm). Sprinkle in 2 teaspoons of the salt. Cover and bring to a boil.

2. Meanwhile, place the cashews and vegetable broth in a high-speed blender and blend until completely smooth, scraping the sides occasionally with a spatula to get everything.

3. When the potatoes have come to a boil, lower the heat to a simmer, uncover, and cook for about 12 minutes, until fork tender. Drain the potatoes and return them to the pot. Mash them with a potato masher to break them up a bit. Add half of the cashew mixture, the coconut oil, remaining ¾ teaspoon salt, and pepper to taste. Mash with a potato masher until relatively smooth and no big chunks are left.

4. Add the remaining cashew mixture, mix it in, and use a hand blender on high speed to whip the mashed potatoes. They should become very smooth, fluffy, and creamy. Taste for salt and pepper along the way, transfer to a serving bowl, and serve!

For roasted red pepper mash: Add 3 roasted red peppers (from a jar or homemade) to the cashew mixture and blend as described in step 2.

For pesto mash: Stir ½ cup (135 g) pesto (page 56) into the classic mashed potatoes after whipping them in step 4.

For garlic mash: Preheat a small pan over low heat. Sauté ¼ cup (35 g) minced garlic in ¼ cup (60 ml) olive oil for about 2 minutes. Stir the garlic oil into the classic mashed potatoes after whipping them in step 4.

I Can Cook Vegan

Miso-Glazed Roasted Carrots

Make your carrots sing with yummy, ferment-y, salty miso and sweet autumnal maple. This dish is especially gorgeous when made with rainbow carrots, so get yourself to a farmers' market—stat!

Ingredients

Serves 4 to 6

3   tablespoons mellow white miso
3   tablespoons warm water
3   tablespoons olive oil
1   tablespoon pure maple syrup
½   teaspoon salt
½   teaspoon red pepper flakes
2   pounds (910 g) carrots, peeled and cut in half lengthwise
¼   cup (25 g) sliced scallions (white and light green parts only)

1. Preheat the oven to 400°F (205°C). Spray two large rimmed baking sheets with nonstick cooking spray.

2. In a large mixing bowl, combine the miso, warm water, olive oil, maple syrup, salt, and red pepper flakes and use a fork to stir them together. Add the carrots and toss to coat. Divide the carrots between the prepared baking sheets and arrange them in a single layer. Bake for about 20 minutes, then flip the carrots, rotate the pans, and bake for an additional 10 minutes, or until beautifully caramelized.

3. To serve, place the carrots on a serving platter and garnish with scallions.

I Can Cook Vegan

Ginger Sweet-Potato Mash

Creamy lush sweet potatoes are elevated to Thanksgiving table status with a little ginger and a dash of cinnamon. But don't just save these for Thanksgiving—they're wonderful with tofu and greens any night of the week. Or morning. Or afternoon.

Ingredients

2   pounds (910 g) sweet potatoes, peeled and cut into 1-inch (2.5 cm) chunks
1   tablespoon grated fresh ginger
¼   teaspoon ground cinnamon
2   tablespoons refined coconut oil
2   tablespoons pure maple syrup
1   teaspoon salt

Serves 4 to 6

1. Place the sweet potatoes in a 4-quart (3.8 L) pot and add enough water to submerge them by 2 inches (5 cm). Cover the pot and bring to a boil, then lower the heat and let simmer for 5 minutes, until fork tender.

2. Drain the sweet potatoes. Add the grated ginger, cinnamon, coconut oil, maple syrup, and salt. Use a potato masher to mash until creamy. Taste for salt and seasoning, then serve.

Caulipots

Yes, more mashed potatoes. But this is a more cruciferous, lower-fat way to have your carb-y fave every night of the week!

Ingredients

1½ pounds (680 g) Yukon Gold potatoes, cut into ¾-inch (2 cm) chunks
4   cups (540 g) cauliflower florets
2   tablespoons refined coconut oil
½   teaspoon salt, plus more, if needed
    Freshly ground black pepper

Serves 4

1. Place the potatoes in a 4-quart (3.8 L) pot with enough cold salted water to submerge them by about 4 inches (10 cm). This way, the cauliflower will be submerged when you add it. Bring the potatoes to a boil, then add the cauliflower and lower the heat to a simmer. Let simmer for about 15 minutes, until the potatoes and cauliflower are tender.

2. Pour off most of the water, reserving about ¼ cup (60 ml) liquid in the pot. Add the oil, salt, and pepper to taste and use a potato masher to mash the potato and cauliflower really, really well. Taste for salt and serve.

On the Side

Maple-Mustard Brussels Sprouts with Radicchio and Pecans

With so few ingredients, the brussels sprouts get caramelized, sweet, and savory; red pepper flakes add a little bit of heat. The radicchio is a fresh and fancy touch, because who doesn't need a little purple on their dinner plate?

Ingredients

½ cup (120 ml) pure maple syrup
½ cup (120 ml) Dijon mustard
¼ cup (60 ml) olive oil
1 teaspoon salt
1 teaspoon red pepper flakes
2 pounds (910 g) brussels sprouts, trimmed and sliced in half
1 cup (100 g) raw pecans
2 small heads radicchio, shaved into thin slices

Serves 8

1. Preheat the oven to 400°F (205°C). Spray two large rimmed baking sheets with nonstick cooking spray.

2. In a large mixing bowl, stir together the maple syrup, mustard, olive oil, salt, and red pepper flakes. Add the brussels sprouts and toss to coat. Divide between the prepared baking sheets and arrange the sprouts in a single layer. Bake for about 20 minutes, then flip the sprouts, rotate the pans, and bake for an additional 10 minutes, or until caramelized.

3. In the meantime, preheat a cast-iron skillet over moderate heat. Toast the pecans, flipping occasionally, about 5 minutes. Remove from the heat and let cool. Roughly chop.

4. To serve, place the brussels sprouts on a serving platter and sprinkle with the pecans. Garnish with the shaved radicchio.

I Can Cook Vegan

Savory Herb Bread Pudding

This pudding tastes like Stove Top Stuffing Mix, which makes it a perfect base for Thanksgiving-y things or when you want a change from traditional mashed potatoes (when is that again?). Slightly stale bread works best, but if yours isn't there yet, lightly toast the cubes for 5 minutes or so before proceeding with the recipe.

Ingredients

¼ cup (60 ml) olive oil, plus more for the baking dish
1 small yellow onion, chopped into medium dice
2 ribs celery, thinly sliced
Salt
2 teaspoons onion powder
½ teaspoon dried sage
3 tablespoons chopped fresh thyme
1 tablespoon chopped fresh rosemary
Freshly ground black pepper
1 loaf bakery white bread, cubed
2 cups (480 ml) vegetable broth
Chopped fresh flat-leaf parsley, for serving

Serves 4 to 6

1. Preheat the oven to 400°F (205°C). Lightly grease a 10-inch (25 cm) square baking dish.

2. Preheat a 6-quart (5.7 L) pot over medium heat. Sauté the onion and celery in the olive oil with a pinch of salt until onion is lightly browned, about 7 minutes. Stir in the onion powder, sage, thyme, rosemary, 1 teaspoon salt, and several dashes of pepper and turn off the heat.

3. Put the bread cubes in a large mixing bowl. Add the cooked vegetable mixture and toss to thoroughly coat. Pour in the vegetable broth, ½ cup (120 ml) at a time, mixing well after each addition. The bread should be moist but not soggy, so you may not need to add all the broth.

4. Transfer the stuffing mixture to the prepared casserole dish. Cover with aluminum foil and bake for 20 minutes. Uncover and bake for an additional 10 minutes. Remove from the oven and let cool a bit before serving.

I Can Cook Vegan

Turmeric Garlic Rice

This is so easy I'm embarrassed to call it a recipe, but I make garlic rice dozens of times a year, and as simple as it is, I absolutely can't resist it. It's yellow garlicky rice—what's not to like about that? I use this recipe often with curries but also in rice and beans or with a tomato-y stew.

Ingredients

6   cloves garlic, minced
2   tablespoons refined coconut oil
1   teaspoon ground turmeric
2   cups (360 g) white basmati rice
1   teaspoon salt

Serves 4

1.   Preheat a 4-quart (3.8 L) pot over medium heat. Sauté the garlic in the coconut oil until fragrant, about a minute. Add the turmeric, rice, 2½ cups (600 ml) water, and the salt and give them a gentle stir. Cover, raise the heat up to medium-high, and bring to a boil.

2.   Once the water is boiling, turn the heat as low as it will go and simmer for 15 to 20 minutes. The water should be completely absorbed.

3.   Turn the heat off and let sit for an additional 15 minutes, still covered. Fluff with a fork and serve.

Coconut Creamed Corn

Coconut brings out all the a-MAIZE-ing flavor of corn in a down-home side dish that's thick, creamy, and buttery. I make it with frozen corn, but if you have the gumption to try it with fresh, that would probably be even more delish, so go for it.

Ingredients

Serves 4

3   tablespoons refined coconut oil
3   tablespoons all-purpose flour
1   (15-ounce/430 g) can
        coconut milk
1   (12-ounce/340 g) package
        frozen corn, thawed
½   teaspoon salt
        Freshly ground black pepper

1.   Preheat a 4-quart (3.8 L) pot over medium heat. Melt the coconut oil in the pot, then sprinkle in the flour. Use a wooden spoon to stir and toast the flour mixture (it should be thick and pasty) for about 3 minutes.

2.   Slowly pour in the coconut milk in a steady stream, mixing it into the flour mixture as you go. Continue to cook until the sauce thickens, about 5 minutes.

3.   Add the corn and salt. Cook until heated through. Season with pepper, taste for salt, and serve.

Chapter

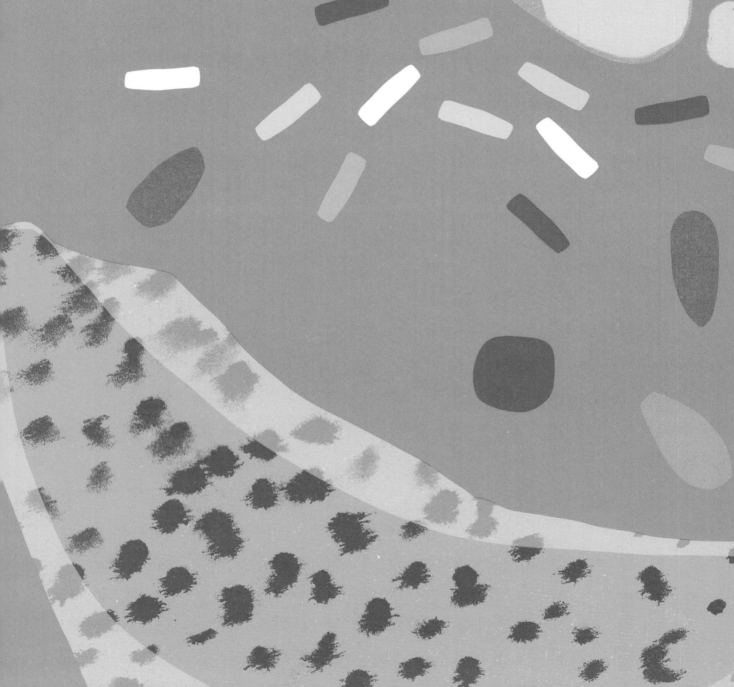

8

Sweets

Mission: Get baking! Tempt your friends and family with fresh-from-the-oven baked goods. Learn to carefully follow instructions, mix batters, and invert muffins out of their pans. Test your patience by actually waiting for those cupcakes to cool before spreading on the frosting. Baking is a whole other world, and this is your entry into it.

You don't have to become a master baker, but it wouldn't hurt to master a few things! The recipes herein are designed to get your sweet tooth started, from cookies to pancakes (because, come on, that's basically dessert).

Vegan baking has become quite commonplace over the past decade or so, and I think the reason for that is that it's easier. The ingredients are pantry-friendly, the methods are straightforward, and the results are excellent. Vegan cupcakes practically grow on trees nowadays!

Equipment must-haves

You won't need any complicated equipment here—I do most of my mixing with a fork. But you will need a few things.

Oven thermometer:
Your oven lies to you. Make sure that the temperature is correct and everything will fall into place.

A few good-size mixing bowls:
Although most of the recipes in this chapter are one-bowl, it never hurts to have a collection of varying sizes, from tiny to this-gigantic-bowl-doesn't-fit-anywhere.

A good strong fork with a longish handle:
Make sure you have a favorite one that doesn't bend.

A mesh sifter:
Because that confectioners' sugar and baking powder won't unclump themselves.

Dry measuring cups:
Stainless steel with strong handles that will last forever.

A few sets of measuring spoons:
Because you will lose that one-fourth teaspoon, I guarantee it. Again, stainless steel and strong.

I Can Cook Vegan

Baking vessels you will need

I never bake with glass or silicone. All recipes in the book were tested with metal baking pans, and I recommend using the same.

1 (8-inch/20 cm) square baking dish

2 (18-inch/46 cm) rimmed baking sheets

Bundt pan or mini Bundt pan

Standard muffin pans (or jumbo, for big muffins, if you like) for cupcakes

2 (8-inch/20 cm) springform pans, for easy release of your precious cakes

Oh, and parchment paper and cooking spray!

Some ingredients that vegan bakers use

Ground flax seeds
Normal flax seeds are brown, so I prefer golden because, as the name suggests, they have a light color that blends nicely into your pastries. It's also sometimes called flax meal. Keep it refrigerated once the package is opened.

Milks
I tested these recipes with most of the popular milks on the market—almond, soy, coconut blend (NOT coconut milk from a can). And they all worked! Unless specified, use your fave milk in recipes that call for it. The only caution I have is that rice milk lacks fat and sometimes makes baked goods a little lighter.

Refined coconut oil
Virgin coconut oil will lend a coconut flavor to pastries, so I prefer refined. It has a neutral, even buttery, flavor and bakes up beautifully. Do be aware of the temperature requirements for each recipe—sometimes it's melted, sometimes it's at room temp, sometimes it doesn't matter. But follow the recipes for best results. To melt coconut oil, place the jar in hot water, or scoop some into a microwave-safe bowl and heat for about 30 seconds, then let it melt the rest of the way.

Apple cider vinegar
Like buttermilk, vinegar reacts with baking powder as a powerful leavening agent. So I always have some in my baking pantry.

Classic Chocolate Chip Cookies

Let's bake from the very beginning, the very best place to bake. The first question is what does everyone want in a chocolate chip cookie? Butteriness, a touch of brown sugar, crispness but also chewiness, vanilla, and what do you call those things? Oh yeah, chocolate chips. In this recipe, coconut oil creates buttery depth, a little cornstarch makes the cookies crisp on the bottom and chewy inside, and the rest—brown sugar, vanilla, chocolate chips—is already vegan so we're good to go! One crucial rule for all drop cookies is not to overbake them. The tops should still be soft and the bottoms should be just this side of golden brown when you take them out of the oven. Then make sure you get them off the baking sheet within 2 minutes or so, because they do continue to bake on the hot pan even once they're out of the oven.

Ingredients

½   cup (120 ml) refined coconut oil, at room temperature
⅓   cup (75 g) packed light brown sugar
⅓   cup (65 g) granulated sugar
¼   cup (60 ml) unsweetened nondairy milk
1   tablespoon cornstarch
2   teaspoons pure vanilla extract
1⅓ (145 g) cups all-purpose flour
½   teaspoon salt
½   teaspoon baking soda
½   cup (85 g) semisweet chocolate chips

Makes 24 cookies

1.   Preheat the oven to 350°F (175°C). Lightly grease two large baking sheets.

2.   In a large mixing bowl, use a fork to beat together the coconut oil and both sugars until well combined and somewhat resembling applesauce, about 2 minutes. Add the milk and cornstarch and beat again, for another minute or so. Mix in the vanilla.

3.   Add about half the flour, the salt, and baking soda and mix well. Add the remainder of the flour along with the chocolate chips and mix well until it looks like, well, cookie dough.

4.   Scoop about 2 tablespoons of the dough onto the prepared cookie sheets in rounded spoonfuls about 2 inches (5 cm) apart. Flatten them gently with your hands. Bake for 10 to 12 minutes, until the bottoms of the cookies are golden brown.

5.   Let cool on the sheets for 3 minutes or so, then transfer to cooling racks to cool the rest of the way.

I Can Cook Vegan

Chocolate Chunk–Rosemary Chocolate Cookies

Chocolate has been waiting its whole life to be coupled with rosemary! It took the new millennium to make it happen. A few cookbooks ago I created a rosemary chocolate chip cookie and it has been one of my most popular recipes ever. It's like a chocolatey kiss in a forest! This time around, I upped the chocolate game. The dough is chocolate and we are using broken-up chocolate chunks to create the chips, for bigger chocolate bites. To create the chocolate chunks, use a chef's knife to cut through the chocolate bar in one swift motion, and repeat until you have chunks that are around ¼ inch (6 mm) thick. You can also use the crumbs that form; just throw everything in when the recipe says you should.

Ingredients

Makes 24 cookies

- ½ cup (120 ml) refined coconut oil, at room temperature
- 2 tablespoons lightly packed, chopped fresh rosemary
- ⅓ cup (65 g) granulated sugar
- ⅓ cup (75 g) packed light brown sugar
- ¼ cup (60 ml) unsweetened nondairy milk
- 1 tablespoon ground flax seeds
- 2 teaspoons pure vanilla extract
- 1 cup (125 g) all-purpose flour
- ⅓ cup (30 g) unsweetened cocoa powder, sifted if clumpy
- ½ teaspoon salt
- ½ teaspoon baking soda
- 1 (4-ounce/115 g) dark chocolate bar, broken into chunks (see headnote)

1. Preheat the oven to 350°F (175°C). Lightly grease two large baking sheets.

2. In a large mixing bowl, use a fork to beat together the coconut oil, rosemary, and both sugars until well combined and somewhat resembling apple-sauce, about 2 minutes. Add the milk and flax seeds and beat again, for another minute or so. Mix in the vanilla.

3. Add about half the flour, the salt, and baking soda and mix well. Add the remainder of the flour along with the choco-late chunks and mix well until it looks like, well, cookie dough.

4. Scoop about 2 tablespoons of dough onto the prepared cookie sheets in rounded spoonfuls about 2 inches (5 cm) apart. Flatten them gently with your hands. Bake for 10 to 12 minutes, until the cookies are crisp on the bottom but still soft on top.

5. Let cool on the sheets for 3 minutes or so, then transfer to cooling racks to cool the rest of the way.

I Can Cook Vegan

Oatmeal-Walnut Chocolate Chip Cookies

Toasty, oaty, nutty cookies, studded with chocolate and a little bit salty. These are a perfect lunch box treat!

Ingredients

½   cup (120 ml) refined coconut oil, at room temperature
½   cup (110 g) lightly packed light brown sugar
½   cup (100 g) granulated sugar
½   cup (120 ml) unsweetened nondairy milk
1   tablespoon ground flax seeds
1   teaspoon pure vanilla extract
1   cup (125 g) all-purpose flour
½   teaspoon baking powder
½   teaspoon baking soda
¾   teaspoon salt
½   cup (60 g) roughly chopped walnuts
¾   cup (130 g) semisweet chocolate chips
2   cups (180 g) rolled oats

Makes 24 cookies

1. Preheat the oven to 350°F (175°C). Lightly grease two large baking sheets.

2. In a large mixing bowl, use a fork to beat together the coconut oil and sugars until well combined and somewhat resembling applesauce, about 2 minutes. Add the milk and ground flax seeds and beat again, for another minute or so. Mix in the vanilla.

3. Add the flour, baking powder, baking soda, and salt and mix well. Add the walnuts, chocolate chips, and oats and use your hands to mix until everything is evenly distributed and a stiff dough is formed.

4. Scoop about 3 tablespoons of dough onto the prepared cookie sheets in rounded spoonfuls about 2 inches (5 cm) apart. Flatten gently with your hands. Bake for 10 to 12 minutes, until the bottoms of the cookies are golden brown.

5. Let cool on the sheets for 3 minutes or so, then transfer to cooling racks to cool the rest of the way.

I Can Cook Vegan

Raspberry Pretzel Thumbprints with Chocolate Drizzle

These unique cookies will satisfy all your salty and sweet cravings, and they're really pretty to boot! Pretzel-studded cookies with a ruby center and chocolate ribbons—they're like a holiday treat no matter what time of year you're baking them.

Ingredients

½ cup (120 ml) canola oil
¾ cup (150 g) granulated sugar
⅓ cup (75 g) packed brown sugar
¼ cup (60 ml) unsweetened nondairy milk
1½ teaspoons pure vanilla extract
1⅔ cups (205 g) all-purpose flour
½ cup (50 g) unsweetened cocoa powder
3 tablespoons cornstarch
1 teaspoon baking powder
¼ teaspoon salt
1 cup (40 g) thin pretzel sticks
½ cup (120 ml) seedless raspberry jam
½ cup (85 g) semisweet chocolate chips

Makes 24 cookies

1. Preheat the oven to 350°F (175°C). Lightly grease two large baking sheets.

2. In a large bowl, beat together the oil, both sugars, milk, and vanilla. Sift in the flour, cocoa powder, cornstarch, baking powder, and salt. Stir to form a thick, stiff dough.

3. Spread the pretzels out on a large cutting board and cover them with parchment paper. Roll a rolling pin over them to crush them into bits and pieces.

4. Scoop up walnut-size pieces of dough, moisten your hands, and roll the dough into a ball. Then place the pieces of dough on the pretzel pieces, rolling them around so that the pieces adhere. Put the pretzel-coated balls of dough on the prepared cookie sheets about 1½ inches (4 cm) apart.

5. Use your pinky to make a deep indent in the center of each ball of dough. Use a teaspoon to fill each indent with about a teaspoon of jam. Bake for 14 to 16 minutes, until golden on the edges and lightly browned on the bottoms.

6. Transfer the cookies to a cooling rack and wait until completely cool to proceed.

7. Place the cooling rack of cookies over or in the sink. Using a microwave or double boiler, melt the chocolate chips, then drizzle the melted chocolate over the cooled cookies, letting the excess fall into the sink for easy cleanup. Let set in a cool room or in the fridge for about 30 minutes before serving.

I Can Cook Vegan

Chocolate Pistachio Biscotti

Biscotti are somehow very fancy, especially if there are pistachios involved. But they're also secretly very easy, and truth be told, they're the cookie I make if I'm feeling a little lazy. Who has time to spoon cookies onto a baking sheet when you can just form two gigantic cookies and go about your business! Yes, you have to slice them up, but we will get to that. This classic, favorite combo is enhanced with a little almond extract. The resulting biscotti are yummy and stunning, too, with gorgeous green pistachios peeking out, so make them for your afternoon coffee, but also wrap some up with twine for a pretty cookie gift.

Ingredients

⅓ cup (75 ml) unsweetened nondairy milk
2 tablespoons ground flax seeds
¾ cup (150 g) sugar
½ cup (120 ml) refined coconut oil, melted
1 teaspoon pure vanilla extract
¼ teaspoon almond extract
1½ cups (190 g) all-purpose flour
⅓ cup (30 g) unsweetened cocoa powder
2 tablespoons cornstarch
2 teaspoons baking powder
½ teaspoon salt
1 cup (130 g) shelled pistachios

Makes 18 cookies

1. Preheat the oven to 350°F (175°C). Lightly grease a large baking sheet.

2. In a large mixing bowl, whisk together the milk and flax seeds. Beat in the sugar, melted coconut oil, and both extracts. Mix for about 2 minutes, until relatively smooth.

3. Sift in half of the flour along with the cocoa powder, cornstarch, baking powder, and salt. Stir just until incorporated; a few dry spots are okay. Mix in the pistachios, then add the remaining flour and use your hands to form a stiff dough.

4. Divide the dough in half and shape into two 5 by 3-inch (12 by 7.5 cm) logs. Transfer the logs to the prepared baking sheet and bake for 25 minutes, until puffed up. Let cool on the cookie sheet for 30 to 40 minutes, until firm and just warm to the touch.

5. Transfer the loaves to a cutting board. Use a serrated bread knife to slice the loaves crosswise into 1-inch (2.5 cm) slices. Do this in one swift motion; do not saw the cookies, just press down on the knife.

6. Place each cookie cut side down on the cookie sheet. Bake for 20 minutes more, flipping the cookies halfway through. Transfer to a cooling rack to cool completely.

Lemon Almond Biscotti

Biscotti for the lemon lover in your life! Lemon and almond in a crispy package; it's like you're sitting outside an espresso shop in Little Italy, except without all the honking taxis. This is a fun recipe where you get to drizzle icing all over everything, so have your inner child or your actual child at the ready.

Ingredients

- ¼ cup (60 ml) unsweetened nondairy milk
- ¼ cup (60 ml) fresh lemon juice
- 2 tablespoons ground flax seeds
- ¾ cup (150 g) sugar
- ½ cup (120 ml) refined coconut oil, melted
- 2 tablespoons grated lemon zest
- 1 teaspoon pure vanilla extract
- ¼ teaspoon almond extract
- 1⅔ cups (205 g) all-purpose flour
- 2 tablespoons cornstarch
- 2 teaspoons baking powder
- ½ teaspoon salt
- 1 cup (95 g) sliced almonds
- 1 recipe Lemon Glaze (page 264)

Makes 18 cookies

1. Preheat the oven to 350°F (175°C). Lightly grease a large baking sheet.

2. In a large mixing bowl, whisk together the milk, lemon juice, and flax seeds. Beat in the sugar, melted coconut oil, lemon zest, and both extracts. Mix for about 2 minutes, until relatively smooth.

3. Sift in half of the flour along with the cornstarch, baking powder, and salt. Stir just until incorporated; a few dry spots are okay. Mix in the almonds, then add the remaining flour and use your hands to form a stiff dough.

4. Divide the dough in half and shape into two 5 by 3-inch (12 by 7.5 cm) logs. Transfer the logs to the prepared baking sheet and bake for 25 minutes, until puffed up. Let cool on the cookie sheet for 30 to 40 minutes, until firm and just warm to the touch.

5. Transfer the loaves to a cutting board. Use a serrated bread knife to slice crosswise into 1-inch (2.5 cm) slices. Do this in one swift motion; do not saw the cookies, just press down on the knife.

6. Place each cookie cut side down on the cookie sheet. Bake for 20 minutes more, flipping the cookies halfway through. Transfer to a cooling rack to cook completely.

7. Place the cooling rack of cookies over the sink. Use a spoon to drizzle the lemon glaze over the cooled cookies, letting the excess fall into the sink for easy cleanup. Let set in a cool room or in the fridge for about 30 minutes before serving.

Walnut Brownies

Brownies. Just what the doctor ordered! Okay, probably not. But everyone else ordered them. My favorite kind of brownie is somewhere between fudgy and cakey. It's got a crackly top, you need a glass of milk when you eat it, it is as chocolatey as can be, and it's studded with walnuts. And now it can be your favorite, too!

Ingredients

½ cup (85 g) semisweet chocolate chips
⅓ cup (75 ml) refined coconut oil
⅔ cup (135 g) sugar
⅓ cup (75 ml) unsweetened applesauce
1 tablespoon cornstarch
1½ teaspoons pure vanilla extract
1 cup (125 g) all-purpose flour
½ teaspoon baking powder
3 tablespoons unsweetened cocoa powder, sifted if clumpy
½ teaspoon salt
1 cup (120 g) coarsely chopped walnuts

Makes 9 brownies

1. Preheat the oven to 350°F (175°C). Lightly grease an 8-inch (20 cm) square brownie pan.

2. Melt the chocolate chips and coconut oil and pour them into a large mixing bowl. Let cool to room temperature; this should take about 10 minutes. In the meantime, measure everything else out.

3. Beat the sugar, applesauce, and cornstarch into the melted chocolate. Mix until very smooth. Stir in the vanilla.

4. Mix in half the flour, the baking powder, cocoa powder, and salt. Fold in the walnuts, then add the remaining flour and mix until no dry clumps are left.

5. Transfer the batter to the prepared pan and use a spatula to spread it out evenly. Bake for 18 to 20 minutes, until the edges are lightly pulling away from the pan. Place the pan on a cooling rack and slice the brownies when cool.

Pecan Sandies

If your thing is pure, unadulterated toasty pecan goodness, you've come to the right place. More like a shortbread than a cookie, these are tender, crumbly (thus, "sandies"), and melt in your mouth. Folks have been known to toss them in powdered sugar, so you can try that, but I prefer to keep my black clothes black.

Ingredients

Makes 18 cookies

⅔ cup (165 ml) refined coconut oil, softened
½ cup (100 g) sugar
¼ cup (60 ml) rice milk (or fave nondairy milk)
2 teaspoons pure vanilla extract
2 cups (255 g) all-purpose flour
½ teaspoon salt
¼ teaspoon allspice
1 cup (120 g) finely chopped pecans

1. Preheat the oven to 325°F (165°C). Line 2 rimmed baking sheets with parchment paper.

2. In a large mixing bowl, use a fork or electric mixer to beat together the coconut oil and sugar until well combined and somewhat resembling apple-sauce.

3. Add the milk and beat again, for another minute or so. Mix in the vanilla.

4. Add about half the flour, the salt, and allspice and mix well. Add the remaining flour and the pecans and continue to mix until a stiff dough forms. Refrigerate for about 20 minutes.

5. Form dough into walnut-size balls. Flatten gently with your hands. Place on the prepared baking sheets and bake for 16 to 18 minutes, until bottoms are golden brown.

6. Let cool on sheets for 3 minutes or so, then transfer to cooling racks to cool the rest of the way.

I Can Cook Vegan

Chocolate Layer Cake

A few times a decade you will be called upon to make a layer cake. It might be for a birthday or a retirement. It might be for a date night where it's just you and the Lifetime Real Women channel. Whatever. Now that we've established that you are going to make a layer cake, this is the one to make. Olive oil creates a moist and delicate crumb and enhances the chocolatiness, like, wow! The frosting is thick and creamy but almost like a milk chocolate, so not too rich. It's just a real great chocolate cake.

For the cake

- 2 cups (480 ml) unsweetened nondairy milk
- 2 teaspoons apple cider vinegar
- 1½ cups (300 g) sugar
- ⅔ cup (165 ml) olive oil
- 2 teaspoons pure vanilla extract
- ½ teaspoon almond extract
- 2 cups (250 g) all-purpose flour
- ⅔ cup (65 g) unsweetened cocoa powder
- 1 tablespoon baking powder
- ½ teaspoon salt

For the chocolate frosting

- 12 ounces (340 g) extra-firm silken tofu (the vacuum-packed kind)
- 1 cup (240 ml) coconut milk
- 2 tablespoons agave
- 1 teaspoon pure vanilla extract
- ¼ teaspoon salt
- 12 ounces (340 g) semisweet chocolate chips

Makes one 8-inch (20 cm) cake

1. Make the cake: Preheat the oven to 350°F (175°C). Lightly spray two 8-inch (20 cm) springform pans with nonstick cooking spray. Whisk together the milk and vinegar in a large bowl and set aside for a few minutes to curdle. Add the sugar, oil, vanilla, and almond extract and mix well.

2. In a separate bowl, sift together the flour, cocoa powder, baking powder, and salt. Whisk the dry ingredients into the the wet ingredients in three batches, mixing well after each addition. Beat until the batter is smooth.

3. Divide the batter between the pans and bake for 32 to 35 minutes, until a toothpick inserted into the center comes out clean. Let cool completely before releasing the cakes from the pans.

4. Meanwhile, make the chocolate frosting: In a blender, combine the tofu, coconut milk, agave, vanilla, and salt. Puree until completely smooth.

5. In a microwave or double boiler, melt the chocolate chips. Remove from heat and let cool for 5 minutes, stirring occasionally.

6. Add the chocolate to the tofu mixture and blend until well combined. Use the spatula to scrape down the sides of the blender every so often.

7. Transfer to a bowl and let chill for about 1 hour, until it's cool and set but spreadable. Bring to room temperature if it seems too stiff.

8. Place one cake upside down on a large plate so that the flat side is facing up. Use a palette knife or spatula (or, heck, the back of a tablespoon) to spread a third of the frosting on top of the cake to the edge. Place the other cake on top of the frosted cake, flat side down. Frost the top and sides of the cake. Refrigerate for about an hour before serving.

I Can Cook Vegan

Chocolate Cupcakes with Peanut Butter Frosting

Chocolate and peanut butter is someone's favorite combination. I forgot who. Oh, that's right, everyone!

For the cupcakes

1	cup (240 ml) unsweetened nondairy milk
1	teaspoon apple cider vinegar
¾	cup (150 g) granulated sugar
⅓	cup (75 ml) refined coconut oil, melted
1½	teaspoons pure vanilla extract
1	cup (125 g) all-purpose flour
⅓	cup (30 g) unsweetened cocoa powder
¾	teaspoon baking soda
½	teaspoon baking powder
¼	teaspoon salt

For the peanut butter frosting

½	cup (135 g) smooth natural peanut butter, at room temperature
¼	teaspoon salt
1	teaspoon pure vanilla extract
2½	cups (250 g) confectioners' sugar (sifted if clumpy)
¼	cup (60 ml) warm almond milk, plus an extra splash, if needed
2	tablespoons refined coconut oil, melted

Makes 12 cupcakes

1. Make the cupcakes: Preheat the oven to 350°F (175°C) and line a muffin pan with paper liners.

2. Whisk together the milk and vinegar in a large bowl and set aside for a few minutes to curdle. Add the sugar, coconut oil, and vanilla to the milk mixture and beat until foamy.

3. In a separate bowl, sift together the flour, cocoa powder, baking soda, baking powder, and salt. Add the dry ingredients to the wet ingredients in two batches and beat until no large lumps remain (a few tiny lumps are okay).

4. Lightly spray the liners with nonstick cooking spray and pour the batter into the liners, filling them three-fourths of the way. Bake for 18 to 20 minutes, until a toothpick inserted into the center comes out clean. Transfer to a cooling rack and let cool completely.

5. Make the frosting: Combine the peanut butter, salt, and vanilla in a large mixing bowl. Add the confectioners' sugar and pour in the almond milk. Use a hand mixer to beat everything together until relatively smooth. Add the coconut oil and beat again. This time the frosting should get really smooth and fall from the blades of the mixer in ribbons. If it seems stiff, add a splash more milk to loosen it up. Seal the bowl with plastic wrap and refrigerate for about 30 minutes.

6. When the cupcakes are cool and the frosting is set, give the frosting a stir with a fork or a hand mixer. Transfer the frosting into a piping bag and pipe it on the cupcakes, or spread the frosting on with the back of a spoon.

Strawberry Lemonade Cupcakes

These cupcakes are like when it's summer and you want something cold and refreshing, but you eat a cupcake instead! The cake is a bright burst of lemon, and the buttercream is only four ingredients and so strawberry-forward. Picture a million strawberry and lemon emojis here.

For the cupcakes

- ¾ cup (150 g) granulated sugar
- 1 cup (240 ml) rice milk, at room temperature (or fave nondairy milk)
- ¼ cup (120 ml) refined coconut oil, melted
- 1 teaspoon pure vanilla extract
- ¼ cup (120 ml) fresh lemon juice
- 1 tablespoon finely grated lemon zest
- 1½ cups (190 g) all-purpose flour
- 1 teaspoon baking powder
- ¼ teaspoon baking soda
- ½ teaspoon salt

For the strawberry buttercream

- 1 cup (165 g) fresh strawberries, chopped, stems removed
- ¾ cup (180 ml) refined coconut oil, softened at room temperature
- 4½ cups (410 g) confectioners' sugar
- 1 teaspoon pure vanilla extract
- 6 strawberries, halved, for decorating

Makes 12 cupcakes

1. Make the cupcakes: Preheat the oven to 350°F (175°C) and line a muffin pan with paper liners.

2. Vigorously beat together sugar, milk, and coconut oil until it resembles applesauce. Mix in vanilla, lemon juice, and lemon zest.

3. Sift in about half the flour, all the baking powder, the baking soda, and the salt. Mix until relatively smooth. Add the remaining flour and mix until smooth and no large lumps remain.

4. Lightly spray the liners with nonstick cooking spray and pour batter into the liners, about three-quarters full. Bake for 16 to 18 minutes, until a toothpick inserted into the center comes out clean. Transfer to a cooling rack and let cool completely.

5. Make the buttercream: In a food processor, puree the strawberries. Transfer to a large mixing bowl and beat with the coconut oil using an electric mixer. Gradually add the confectioners' sugar, scraping the bowl as you go. Add the vanilla and mix until smooth and creamy. If the buttercream seems loose, place in the refrigerator to set a bit, then fluff with a fork.

6. Spread frosting onto cooled cupcakes using the back of a spoon (or your preferred method). Top each cupcake with a strawberry half!

Buckwheat Banana Bread

Buckwheat brings out the best in bananas. It's got a toasty, nutty, wholesome flavor and a soft but rustic texture. It just takes things to a whole other level, so rest assured, if someone else brings banana bread to the potluck, yours will be the recipe everyone asks for. Banana sizes are all over the place, so it's very important to measure mashed bananas and get the correct amount, or your bread could come out wrong. Mash bananas into a measuring cup until you have 1 cup (300 g), which should take 3 average-size bananas. Have some leftover banana? Well, just eat it.

Ingredients

- 1 cup (300 g) mashed very-ripe banana, plus ½ banana, sliced lengthwise, for garnish (pictured on opposite page)
- ¾ cup (150 g) sugar
- ¼ cup (60 ml) refined coconut oil, melted
- 1 cup (240 ml) unsweetened nondairy milk
- 1 teaspoon pure vanilla extract
- 1 cup (125 g) all-purpose flour
- ¾ cup (90 g) buckwheat flour
- ¾ teaspoon baking soda
- ¾ teaspoon salt

Makes 1 loaf

1. Preheat the oven to 350°F (175°C).

2. In a bowl, beat together the mashed bananas, sugar, canola oil, milk, and vanilla.

3. Sift in both flours, the baking soda, and salt and gently mix just to incorporate. It's okay if there is some flour still visible, just be careful not to overmix.

4. Lightly spray an 8 by 4-inch (20 by 10 cm) loaf pan with nonstick cooking spray. Pour the batter into the pan. If you'd like to decorate the top, place the sliced banana cut sides up and lengthwise over the batter.

5. Bake for 55 minutes, until sides are pulling away from the pan. Use a butter knife to test for doneness. Let cool, then invert onto the counter and slice.

Chocolate-Glazed Doughnuts

Are baked doughnuts really doughnuts? Well, not exactly. But this recipe aims to replicate that fried goodness with crispy exterior and moist interior. And what is it about nutmeg that transforms everything into a doughnut? Who knows, who cares. Just be grateful that you can have these adorable doughnuts without breaking out the deep fryer. You will need two doughnut pans, though, so get thee to the internet and get them before starting this recipe. Grease the pans with actual oil, not cooking spray. It will make the doughnuts crispier on the outside! Use a tablespoon to fill the pans. Don't try to fill each doughnut slot in one shot. And be patient, let the doughnuts cool in the pans for at least 10 minutes.

For the doughnuts

2   cups (250 g) all-purpose flour
1¼   cups (240 g) sugar
2   teaspoons cornstarch
2   teaspoons baking powder
½   teaspoon ground nutmeg
½   teaspoon salt
1½   cups (360 ml) unsweetened
        nondairy milk
3   tablespoons refined coconut
        oil, melted, plus extra
        for greasing the pans
2   teaspoons pure vanilla extract

For the chocolate glaze

1   cup (240 ml) nondairy milk
¾   cup (130 g) semisweet
        chocolate chips
1   tablespoon agave

        Sprinkles, for decorating

Makes 24 doughnuts

1.   Preheat the oven to 350°F (175°C). Grease two doughnut pans with refined coconut oil.

2.   In a large mixing bowl, sift together the flour, sugar, cornstarch, baking powder, nutmeg, and salt. Make a well in the center and add the milk, coconut oil, and vanilla. Mix until it's relatively smooth.

3.   Spoon the batter into the baking pans, filling each compartment about three-quarters full. Bake for 18 minutes, until lightly brown and puffy. Let cool in the baking pans and, once you can handle them, invert the doughnuts onto a cooling rack to cool completely.

4.   Make the glaze: Bring the milk to a boil in a small pot. Turn off the heat and add the chocolate chips and agave. Stir with a rubber spatula until melted and smooth.

5.   Dip each doughnut into the warm chocolate, then return them to the cooling rack and decorate with sprinkles. Place in a cool spot to let the chocolate set.

Mini Pumpkin Bundt Cakes with Lemon Glaze

From October until sometime just before Christmas, pumpkin is all that matters. It's a magical and fleeting moment in time and these little cakes are just the thing for it. Not at all fussy or difficult, they're crowd-pleasing and just the complete embodiment of pumpkin season. I would never tell you to purchase a piece of kitchen equipment that you don't actually need. And I know you don't NEED a mini Bundt pan. Who does? However, I am going to try to convince you to get one! Because I want you to slay that Halloween party with these adorable treats. And I want you to make all your Facebook friends see how incredibly successful you are, making cakes they could never ever pull off. If, however, you don't want to listen to me, you can make these in a muffin tin as well. Just bake them for about 20 minutes instead.

For the cakes

- 2 cups (225 g) pumpkin puree
- ½ cup (120 ml) olive oil
- 1¼ cups (250 g) granulated sugar
- ¾ cup (180 ml) unsweetened nondairy milk
- 2 teaspoons pure vanilla extract
- 1¾ cups (225 g) all-purpose flour
- 2 teaspoons baking powder
- 2 teaspoons pumpkin pie spice
- 1 teaspoon salt

For the glaze

- 2 cups (205 g) confectioners' sugar, sifted
- ½ teaspoon pure vanilla extract
- 3 tablespoons fresh lemon juice
- 1 tablespoon refined coconut oil, melted

Makes 6 mini Bundts

1. Make the cakes: Preheat the oven to 350°F (175°C). Lightly grease a mini Bundt pan.

2. In a large mixing bowl, beat together the pumpkin puree, olive oil, sugar, milk, and vanilla until smooth and creamy.

3. Sift in the flour, baking powder, pumpkin pie spice, and salt. Stir until relatively smooth.

4. Spoon the batter into the baking pans, filling each one about three-quarters full. Bake for 26 minutes, until a toothpick inserted into the center comes out clean. The cakes are done when they are firm and puffy on top and lightly pulling away from sides of the pan. Let cool in the baking pan and, once you can handle it, invert the Bundts onto a cooling rack to cool. Flip right side up to cool completely.

5. Make the glaze: Place confectioners' sugar in a large bowl. Add the vanilla, lemon juice, and coconut oil and stir vigorously, until a thick and smooth but pourable icing forms. If it seems too thick, add warm water by the teaspoon until the desired texture is achieved.

6. Pour approximately 2 tablespoons of icing onto each Bundt, letting the excess drip off. Let set in a cool place.

Banana Cinnamon Swirl Muffins

Nothing against a good old, classic banana muffin, but this recipe will have people talking. Big bites of swirly cinnamon remind me of my favorite treat ever, cinnamon raisin bread. This recipe makes jumbo muffins, but if you like, you can make regular-size muffins. Just do two layers of batter and cinnamon mixture instead of three.

For the muffins

- 1½ cups (335 g) mashed banana, from about 3 very ripe bananas (see headnote on page 260)
- ¼ cup (60 ml) almond milk
- ¼ cup (60 ml) unsweetened applesauce
- 2 tablespoons refined coconut oil, melted
- 1 teaspoon pure vanilla extract
- 1½ cups (190 g) all-purpose flour
- 2½ teaspoons baking powder
- ½ cup (100 g) granulated sugar
- ½ teaspoon salt

For the swirl

- ½ cup (110 g) packed dark brown sugar
- 1 tablespoon ground cinnamon
- 2 tablespoons all-purpose flour
- 1 tablespoon refined coconut oil, melted

Makes 6 jumbo muffins

1. Preheat the oven to 350°F (175°C). Grease a jumbo muffin pan and set aside.

2. In a bowl, mix well the mashed bananas, milk, applesauce, coconut oil, and vanilla.

3. In a large mixing bowl, sift together the flour, baking powder, sugar, and salt. Make a well in the center and add the banana mixture. Mix just until no large lumps remain.

4. Make the swirl: In a small bowl, mix together all the swirl ingredients.

5. Into each muffin cup, spoon about two tablespoons of the batter. Sprinkle with a scant tablespoon of the cinnamon mixture. Spoon another layer of batter, and another layer of cinnamon mix. Repeat one more time so you have 3 layers of each. Use a toothpick to lightly swirl in the cinnamon, about 5 times. Add the final amount of batter, and give another 5 swirls.

6. Bake for 22 to 24 minutes, until a toothpick comes out clean and muffins are firm and puffy on top. Let cool in baking pans and, once you can handle the muffins, invert onto a cooling rack to cool completely.

All-Ages Banana French Toast

When I was a waitress I'd notice a breakfast phenomenon. Parents would order for themselves poached eggs and a healthy salad or whatever, then steal half of their children's French toasts. Parents, order your own French toast! There is no shame in it. This version is coated in banana, browns beautifully, and will definitely tempt you to commit grand theft breakfast. For best results, let the sandwich bread sit out overnight and get just a little stale. This will help it to absorb the custard without getting mushy. If you forget to do that, NBD. Simply put the bread in a toaster oven on low for a minute or so. Don't make toast! Just make sure it's a bit dried out. If it changes color, it's gone too long.

Ingredients

Serves 4

- 2 very ripe bananas
- 1½ cups (360 ml) cold rice milk (or preferred nondairy milk)
- 2 tablespoons all-purpose flour
- 2 tablespoons cornstarch
- ¼ teaspoon salt
- 1 teaspoon pure vanilla extract
- 12 pieces sandwich bread
- Coconut oil for the skillet
- Maple syrup and fruit, for serving

1. Preheat a large nonstick skillet (preferably cast-iron) over medium heat.

2. Combine the bananas, milk, flour, cornstarch, salt, and vanilla in a blender and puree until completely smooth. Transfer to a 9 by 13-inch (23 by 33 cm) baking pan.

3. Place half the bread slices in the baking pan, letting them soak for a minute or two.

4. Melt a thin layer of coconut oil on the skillet. Remove bread from the pan, shaking off the excess batter, and place the bread on the skillet.

5. Cook each side of the bread for about 4 minutes, flipping with a thin, flexible spatula. The bread should be golden to medium brown and flecked with darker spots. Transfer to a plate and cover with aluminum foil to keep warm while you soak and cook the second batch.

6. If not serving immediately, preheat the oven to 200°F (90°C) and place French toast in the oven for up to an hour. Serve with maple syrup and fruit (like bananas and blueberries)!

Fluffy Quinoa Pancakes

Putting quinoa in pancakes might seem like a health trend thing, but the only reason I do it is for the crunch. Not for the extra protein, which I get plenty of elsewhere, and not just to level up my vegan—I'm already at level ten. This is simply my favorite way to eat pancakes these days! The crunch gives me life. The quinoa should be cooked al dente for the best experience. And I like red quinoa for the prettiest contrast. First, make sure your quinoa is cooked according to package directions and cooled. Then proceed with the recipe. To cool quinoa quickly without overcooking it, spread onto a baking sheet and place in the refrigerator.

Ingredients

Makes 8 pancakes

- 1½ cups (190 g) all-purpose flour
- 1 tablespoon baking powder
- 1 teaspoon salt
- 2 tablespoons sugar
- 1¼ cups (300 ml) unsweetened almond milk (or preferred nondairy milk)
- 2 teaspoons apple cider vinegar
- 3 tablespoons canola oil
- ½ teaspoon pure vanilla extract
- 1 cup (200 g) cooked, cooled red quinoa
- Refined coconut oil for the pan

1. In a large mixing bowl, sift together the flour, baking powder, salt, and sugar. Make a well in the center.

2. Add the milk, vinegar, ½ cup (60 ml) water, oil, and vanilla to the well. Stir with a fork until a thick, lumpy batter forms, about a minute. It doesn't need to be smooth, just make sure you incorporate all the ingredients. Fold in the quinoa. Let the batter rest for 10 minutes.

3. Meanwhile, preheat a pan over medium-low heat. Lightly coat the pan with the coconut oil. Add ⅓ cup (75 ml) of the batter for each pancake and cook one side for about 4 minutes, until puffy. Flip the pancakes, adding a new coat of oil to the pan, and cook for another 3 minutes or so. Pancakes should be about ¾ inch (2 cm) thick and golden brown.

4. Transfer pancakes to a large plate and cover with aluminum foil until ready to serve. To reheat, place pancakes on a baking sheet covered with aluminum foil in a 300°F (150°C) oven for 5 minutes or so.

A Few
Staples

No mission here! These are just a few recipes that I use multiple times in the book, all located in one beautiful place.

White Bean Cream Cheese

A creamy spread for bagels and beyond!

Ingredients

Makes 3 cups (720 ml)

¼   cup (60 ml) refined
      coconut oil, melted
1   tablespoon olive oil
3   (15-ounce/430 g) cans navy
      or great northern beans,
      drained and rinsed, or
      3 cups (545 g) cooked beans
2   teaspoons onion powder
2   tablespoons fresh lemon juice
2   teaspoons apple cider vinegar
½   teaspoon salt

In a food processor fitted with a metal blade, place all the ingredients and blend until thick and smooth. Transfer to a container with a cover and chill for at least 30 minutes before using.

Melty Mozzy

If you're going to bake something that requires a cheezy topping, say, manicotti (page 40), this is your simple go-to melty mozz. It cooks up creamy and delicious, with just enough nuance from a little nooch and miso but nothing overpowering.

Ingredients

Makes 2 cups (200 g)

1   cup (120 g) whole unroasted
      cashews (if you don't
      have a high-speed
      blender, see page 24)
2   tablespoons nutritional
      yeast flakes
1   tablespoon mellow white miso
½   teaspoon salt

In a blender, place all ingredients plus ¾ cup (180 ml) water and blend until completely smooth. Scrape down the sides with a rubber spatula to make sure you get everything.

274

Sausage

These sausages have been floating around the internet for years now. The method was first perfected by cookbook author Julie Hasson, then I stole the recipe and ran with it. You can, too! Here's what's going to happen: You're going to mash some beans in a mixing bowl, then mix in the remaining ingredients. Next, you're going to roll 'em in aluminum foil like a Tootsie Roll and steam them. And then, like magic, you will have vegan sausages. Easiest thing in the world!

Ingredients

Makes 4 sausages

½	cup (90 g) cooked navy beans, or about one-third of a 15-ounce (430 g) can, drained and rinsed
1	cup (240 ml) vegetable broth
1	tablespoon olive oil
2	tablespoons soy sauce
1¼	cups (150 g) vital wheat gluten
¼	cup (15 g) nutritional yeast flakes
1	teaspoon granulated garlic
½	teaspoon crushed fennel seed
½	teaspoon red pepper flakes
1	teaspoon sweet paprika
1	teaspoon dried oregano
½	teaspoon dried thyme
	Several dashes freshly ground black pepper

1. Before mixing your ingredients, get the steaming apparatus ready, bring water to a full boil, and prepare 4 sheets of aluminum foil.

2. In a large bowl, mash the beans until no whole ones are left. Throw in all the remaining ingredients and mix with a fork until you have a dough.

3. Divide dough into 4 even portions (an easy way to do this is to split the dough in half, and then split each half again). Form each piece of dough into a 5-inch-long (12 cm) log and wrap in a sheet of foil, like a Tootsie Roll. Don't worry too much about shaping it, it will snap into shape while it's steaming.

4. Place wrapped sausages in steamer and steam for 40 minutes. Let cool, then unwrap or refrigerate until ready to use.

Swizz Cheese

Somehow I discovered that sauerkraut juice plus truffle oil plus a little miso equals Swiss cheese. I don't know, my taste buds sometimes know things before I do! This is the perfect cheese for reubens (page 94), but it's also so wonderful dolloped on veggies like broccoli and cauliflower.

Ingredients

Makes 2½ cups (600 ml)

- 1½ cups whole unroasted cashews (if you don't own a high-speed blender, see page 24)
- ¾ cup (180ml) sauerkraut juice
- 2 tablespoons nutritional yeast flakes
- 2 tablespoons mellow white miso
- 1 tablespoon black truffle oil
- 2 teaspoons onion powder
- 1 teaspoon salt
- ¼ cup (60 ml) organic unrefined coconut oil, melted

In a blender, place all ingredients and blend until completely smooth. Scrape down the sides with a rubber spatula to make sure you get everything.

Eggplant Lardons

Lardons are chunks of fatty bacon. I know, you're like, "People still eat that?!" When made out of bacon they become smoky from the high heat and a dash of smoked paprika—crispy outside, juicy inside, and absolutely addictive. I do use a lot of oil here because, well, it's supposed to be fatty, and eggplant soaks it all up; you can get away with using half the amount, if you want, just expect the eggplant to be a bit dryer outside, and mist with some spray oil during the cooking process.

Ingredients

Makes about 3 cups (300 g)

- 1 large eggplant (about 2 pounds/910 g)
- 2 teaspoons smoked paprika
- 1 teaspoon salt
- ¼ cup (60 ml) olive oil

1. Preheat the oven to 475°F (245°C). Line a rimmed baking sheet with parchment paper.

2. Cut eggplant into ¾-inch (2 cm) pieces. Spread pieces out on the baking sheet. Sprinkle on the paprika and salt. Drizzle half of the olive oil all over the eggplant and toss. Drizzle the remaining oil and toss again.

3. Roast until crispy outside, flipping once, and the eggplant has released lots of moisture, about 20 minutes.

I Can Cook Vegan

Homemade Vegan Mayo

There are so many great vegan mayos on grocery shelves these days, but if the mood strikes, you can make your own!

Ingredients

½   cup (120 ml) unsweetened
      soy milk
1½   tablespoons ground
      golden flax seeds
2   teaspoons sugar
1   teaspoon ground dry mustard
1   teaspoon onion powder
¼   teaspoon salt
1   tablespoon white wine vinegar
1   tablespoon fresh lemon juice
1   cup (240 ml) canola oil

Makes 1½ cups (360 ml)

1. In a blender, combine milk and ground flax seeds. Blend on high speed until the ground flax is barely noticeable and the mixture is frothy, about 1 minute.

2. Add the sugar, dry mustard, onion powder, salt, vinegar, and lemon juice and blend for a few seconds to combine.

3. Now begin to add the oil. With the blender running, use the hole in the lid to stream in 1 tablespoon at a time, blending for about 30 seconds after each addition (if using a high-speed blender like Vitamix, 5 to 10 seconds should do it). Give your blender a break every now and then so that it doesn't heat up the mayo. You should notice it thickening after about half the oil has been added. By the time you've used three-fourths of the oil, it should be spreadable. And with the last addition, you should have a thick mayo. If it seems watery, keep blending.

4. Straight out of the blender, the mayo will probably taste saltier and tangier than you'd like, but the flavors mellow as it sets. Transfer to a glass container, seal tightly, and refrigerate for a few hours. The mayo will thicken even further. Use within a week.

Marinara

I prefer to make my own marinara rather than buy a jar. The scent and, of course, the taste makes the extra time worth it!

Ingredients

Makes 4 cups (960 ml)

1   tablespoon olive oil
1   small yellow onion,
       finely chopped
3   cloves garlic, minced
1   tablespoon brown sugar
1   teaspoon dried thyme
1   teaspoon dried oregano
½   teaspoon crushed red
       pepper flakes (optional,
       if you like a little heat)
    Freshly ground black pepper
1   (24-ounce/680 g) can crushed
       tomatoes with basil
1   teaspoon salt, plus
       more, if needed

Preheat a 2-quart (2 L) pot over medium-low heat. Pour in the olive oil, add the onion, and sauté for about 5 minutes, until lightly browned. Add the garlic and sauté until fragrant, about 30 seconds. Add the brown sugar and cook for about 1 minute, until sugar is dissolved and coating all the onions. Mix in thyme, oregano, red pepper flakes, if desired, and pepper to taste. Add tomatoes and salt and stir everything together. Cover the pot, leaving a little gap for steam to escape, and cook for 15 minutes. Taste for salt and seasoning.

Guacamole

Everyone finds their own way with guacamole. Maybe you like yours a little spicier, or maybe you prefer lemon to lime. This is my go-to! As long as your avocados are perfect, your guac will be perfect, and life will be perfect.

Ingredients

4   ripe avocados
½   teaspoon salt
2   tablespoons fresh lime juice
¼   cup (35 g) minced white onion
¼   cup (55 g) diced tomato
1   tablespoon minced jalapeño
2   tablespoons chopped
         fresh cilantro

Makes 4 cups (940 g)

Slice avocados in half length-wise and remove the pits. Scoop out the flesh and transfer to a mixing bowl. Sprinkle in salt and lime juice. Use an avocado masher or strong fork to give it a good mash. Add the remaining ingredients and mash like crazy, until guacamole is creamy and the tomato has broken up. Taste and adjust flavors, if needed.

Seitan

I have a lot of seitan recipes out there in the world, but this one seems to be the most foolproof and everyone's favorite. It's got neutral flavors and lends itself to every cuisine.

For the broth

8	cups (7.5 L) vegetable broth
6	cloves garlic, smashed
2	bay leaves

For the seitan

2	cups (240 g) vital wheat gluten
¼	cup (15 g) nutritional yeast flakes
¼	cup (25 g) chickpea flour
¼	teaspoon salt
2	teaspoons onion powder
1¼	cups (300 ml) vegetable broth
¼	cup (60 mml) soy sauce
2	teaspoons olive oil

Makes 2 pounds (910 g)

1. Make the broth: Fill a stockpot with the broth, smashed garlic, and bay leaves. Cover and bring to a boil.

2. Make the seitan: In a large bowl, mix together the vital wheat gluten, nutritional yeast, chickpea flour, salt, and onion powder. Make a well in the center and add broth, soy sauce, and olive oil. Mix with a fork and then use your hands to knead for about 3 minutes, until it's a firm dough and everything looks well incorporated.

3. Divide dough into 8 pieces. An easy way to do this is to divide the dough in half, then divide those halves, and then divide those halves. Stretch each piece into a cutlet, pressing the cutlet into the counter to smooth the surface. Let rest until the broth has come to a full boil.

4. Once broth is boiling, lower the heat to a simmer. This is important: the broth should not be at a rolling boil or you risk the seitan getting waterlogged. Add the gluten pieces and partially cover the pot so that steam can escape. Let simmer for 45 minutes, turning the pieces occasionally. Make sure to keep an eye on the heat, because it may start to boil again, in which case, just turn it down a notch to keep at a slow, steady simmer.

5. When done, you can let it cool right in the broth, or remove a portion to use right away. Once cooled, store in a tightly covered container, submerged in broth.

Noochy Baked Tofu

You may want to double this! I also call it "high school tofu" because it was my preferred method for baking tofu in my teenage years. So easy and somehow these simple ingredients create the best baked tofu ever. Add to salads, pastas, bowls, or sandwiches, or just snack on it.

Ingredients

1 (14-ounce/400 g) package extra-firm tofu, drained and chopped into medium dice
1 tablespoons olive oil
1 tablespoon tamari or soy sauce
¼ teaspoon salt
Freshly ground black pepper
2 tablespoons nutritional yeast flakes

Serves 2 to 4

1. Preheat the oven to 350°F (175°C). Line a large rimmed baking sheet with parchment paper.

2. Place the tofu on the baking sheet and drizzle with the oil and tamari. Sprinkle with the salt and several dashes of black pepper. Use your hands to flip and coat. Sprinkle with the nutritional yeast and flip again to coat.

3. Assemble tofu in a single layer. Bake for 20 minutes, until crisp and lightly browned. Use a spatula to flip and bake for 10 more minutes.

Noochy Croutons

This recipe makes more croutons than you'll need for soup, but they keep well for a few weeks and are wonderful for salads or anything else that looks like it could use a crouton.

Ingredients

4 cups (160 g) rustic white bread, crust removed, cut into ¾-inch (2 cm) pieces
2 tablespoons olive oil
½ cup (75 g) nutritional yeast flakes
¼ teaspoon salt

Makes 4 cups (160 g)

1. Preheat the oven to 350°F (175°C). Line a large baking sheet with parchment paper.

2. Place the bread in a large mixing bowl with enough space to toss stuff around. Drizzle with olive oil, tossing to coat. Sprinkle with the yeast and salt and toss. The nutritional yeast won't totally stick, but that's okay. Save the remaining for popcorn or something.

3. Spread onto a baking sheet and bake for 12 to 15 minutes, tossing once. The croutons should be golden and crunchy.

Acknowledgments

Thank you vegans and supporters of vegans.

Thank you to my recipe testers! No thumbprint cookies were harmed in the making of this book.

Thank you to Vanessa Rees and Joshua Foo for taking the beautiful photographs.

Annalea Manalili managed the copyediting, proofreading, and entire process of ensuring this book was as perfect as possible and never gave up on resolving Every Last Query.

Devin Washburn and Philip DiBello from No Ideas created the cool design.

Lucy Sherston illustrated all of this book's amazing art.

Heesang Lee handled the design on the Abrams side, and Denise LaCongo perfected the book's production. Special thanks to you both for uncropping all of the art and letting us do five different proofs of the case.

Thank you Chef Allison Kennedy for holding down the fort while I stormed the castle.

Thank you Marc Gerald for agenting and Michael Sand for championing and Hayley Salmon for overnighting every last printout and proof.

And you, Holly Dolce. There are no words. Except: I promise my next manuscript will be delivered to you at least thirty days early.

Index

I Can Cook Vegan

I Can Cook Vegan

Editor: Holly Dolce
Design: No Ideas
Production Manager: Denise LaCongo

Library of Congress Control Number: 2018958271

ISBN: 978-1-4197-3241-6
eISBN: 978-1-68335-326-3
B&N Signed Edition ISBN: 978-1-4197-4443-3

Printed and bound in China
10 9 8 7 6 5 4 3 2 1

Abrams books are available at special dis-
counts when purchased in quantity for premi-
ums and promotions as well as fundraising or
educational use. Special editions can also be
created to specification. For details, contact
specialsales@abramsbooks.com or the
address below.

Abrams® is a registered trademark of
Harry N. Abrams, Inc.

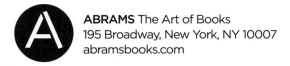

ABRAMS The Art of Books
195 Broadway, New York, NY 10007
abramsbooks.com